THE GRACE WAY

God's path to
successful
Christian living

Cal Bodeutsch

Grace Publications, Inc.
PO Box 9432
Grand Rapids, MI 49509
Phone 616-247-1999 * Fax: 616-241-2542
Website: www.ggfusa.org

THE GRACE WAY. Copyright © 2004 by Calvin Bodeutsch.

Second Edition - 2004

Published by Grace Publications, Inc. PO BOX 9432, Grand Rapids, MI 49509. 616-247-1999. www.ggfusa.org.

ISBN   0-89814-063-3

THE
GRACE
WAY

𝒯o my wife

Karen

**God's grace gift
and helpmeet
with whom I
walk the Grace Way**

Acknowledgments

Many people have influenced me in my walk with God. Beginning with godly parents, Ken and Kay, to our children, Tiersa, Eric and Kristie, each one has contributed, in some way, to my knowledge and dependence upon the grace of God. I am especially indebted to several pastors who have walked with me in the Grace Way. I am grateful to pastors Tim Heath, Harold Collins, Cliff Tulsie and Dan Meininger for their teaching and living out the Grace Way.

Finally, I would like to thank those individuals who have worked with me in the writing of the Grace Way. Lyn Whitham is an editor's editor. She regularly found mistakes in my "perfect" pages. Also helpful was Faith Desmarais in encouraging me to pursue publishing.

All of the praise eventually belongs to God. All that I am and all that I do I owe to the grace of God. "But by the grace of God I am what I am, and His grace toward me did not prove vain; but I labored even more than all of them, yet not I, but the grace of God with me."

(1 Corinthians 15:10 NASB)

TABLE OF CONTENTS

INTRODUCTION..11

Chapter One:
The Legalistic Paradigm....................13

Chapter Two:
Now What? More Grace! 27

Chapter Three:
Getting to Know the Enemy Within 43

Chapter Four:
Trusting God for Godliness....................57

Chapter Five:
Humility..71

Chapter Six:
Know the Word of God........................101

Chapter Seven:
Understand the Word of God............................121

Chapter Eight:
Believe the Word of God................................135

Chapter Nine:
Desire to Obey the Word of God....................151

Chapter Ten:
Empowered to Obey the Word of God..............165

Chapter Eleven:
Obedience to the Word of God........................179

Chapter Twelve:
Bigger than Obedience...................................191

FOREWORD

In THE GRACE WAY, you will find a refreshing new approach regarding how to live the Christian life.

At the beginning of this book, four foundational truths are discussed by the author. These truths make up the core of our understanding of how the Christian life works.

First, we must understand all God's gifts are given by His grace. Second, we must understand the enemy within us, the flesh. Third, we must understand what God requires of us is trust in HIM to produce godliness within us. Finally, the beginning virtue required in us is humility.

In this refreshing approach to godliness, the author develops the Grace Paradigm.

After reading this book, you will find, as I did, a fresh new challenge in your life.

Daniel C. Bultema
Grace Publications

INTRODUCTION

This book is written for new Christians, those who instruct new Christians and those who never got off on the right foot as new Christians. This is a discipleship book written from a grace paradigm. Where some other discipling materials choose to approach the Christian life from a "doing" perspective, this book explains the Christian life from a "being" point of view.

As a pastor and conference speaker I became frustrated with the lack of good discipleship material that explained how the Christian life worked. People have sought my advice over the years on how to live the Christian life. They have already heard "try harder" from pastors, friends and other Christians and it hasn't helped. Sin issues are still unresolved in spite of their best efforts.

I came to the conclusion that trying harder is not the answer, and is in fact, a big part of the problem. Living the Christian life is not a result of our good works any more than was our salvation. Trying hard to save ourselves only pulls us further away from God's grace. In the same vein, trying to live the Christian life in the energy of the flesh only frustrates the grace of God in our life.

At the beginning of this book four foundational truths are discussed. These truths make up the core of our understanding of how the Christian life works. First, we must understand all God's gifts are given by his grace. This includes all of the virtues and blessings that come to us as we yield to the Holy Spirit working within us. Second, we must understand the enemy within us, the flesh. The flesh may take different forms, but each is deadly to the working of the Holy Spirit. Third, we must understand what God requires of us is trust in Him to produce godliness within us. A lack of confidence in God will cause us to be unstable in our relationship with God. Finally, the beginning virtue required in us is humility. Without humility firmly in place, God will resist our self-centered attempts to become more godly.

The second part of the book, beginning at chapter five, provides the basic elements of the Holy Spirit's work in our lives to create and maintain spiritual growth. What is God's responsibility and what is ours? If we try to do God's part, we will fail. If we don't do our part, we will fail. Spiritual growth is not all God's responsibility (let go and let God!), nor is it all ours (do something, even if it is wrong!). We will discover the will of God, related to our spiritual growth, is based on the Word of God.

This book was born of desperation. I was asked by the evangelist Art Fowler to disciple Robbie Knievel, the world-record motorcycle daredevil. Robbie wanted to know how the Christian life worked. Nothing that I could find fit the bill, so I wrote a new lesson each week. Those lessons became the basis for this book.

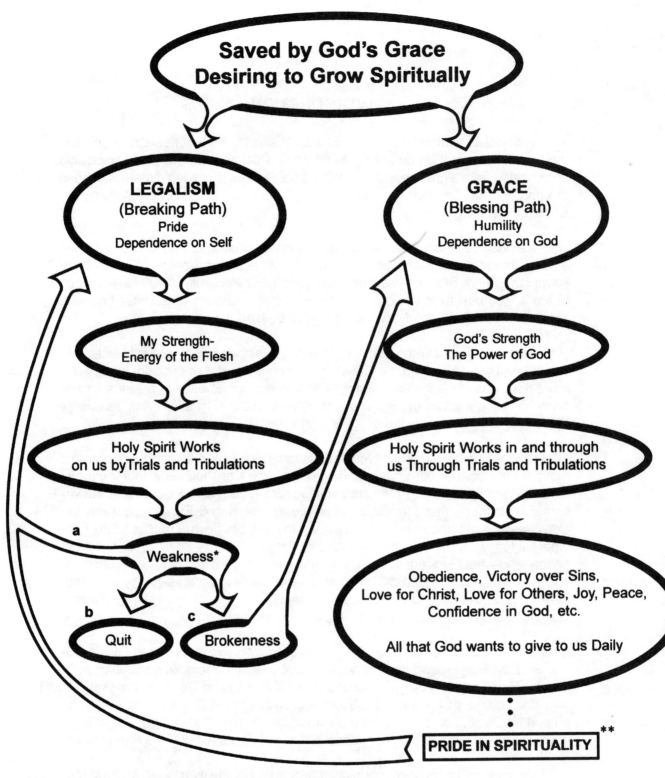

* Once we acknowledge our total weakness we have three choices:
  a. We can try harder living the Christian life under legalism.
  b. We can quit, saying the Christian life doesn't work.
  c. We can be broken by God and begin to live by grace.

** Spiritual pride is always a danger for godly believers, but it is optional. If Satan can't keep you from becoming godly, he will try to destroy it by making you proud of it.

Chart by Eric Bodeutsch

CHAPTER ONE
THE LEGALISTIC PARADIGM

"This book will illustrate two very different paths that the believer seeking spiritual growth may travel."

Two Christians, Bob and John, have two different ideas as to what the Christian life is all about. For Bob Christianity is all about trying to live up to the standards set down in the ten commandments. But for John Christianity is enjoying an intimate relationship with God. Bob is motivated by guilt and fear, John by love. Bob evaluates his spirituality by how many times he has sinned in the past week, while John focuses on getting to know God better. Bob is stuck in the legalistic paradigm.

This book will illustrate two very different paths that the believer seeking spiritual growth may travel. I have found the chart on the opposite page to be helpful in illustrating the difference between the legalistic and grace paradigms. Both begin at the same point where the believer has the desire to grow spiritually, but end up totally different. One ends with, "All that God wants to give to us daily," the other eventually results in frustration and failure. Does it make a difference which path we take in living out the Christian life? Absolutely!

Both pathways begin with salvation by grace through faith. This eliminates unbelievers from the process of spiritual growth. If you have yet to receive God's wonderful gift of eternal life, then why not receive it now? Here is what you must believe: Christ died for our sins and he rose from the grave on the third day (1 Corinthians 15:2-4). The Bible states that the payment for sin is death (Romans 6:23). Jesus Christ paid that payment for you when he died on the cross. Based on the action of Christ, God wants to give you the gift of salvation.

(Your thoughts, impressions and experiences)

13

"God wants to give you the gift of salvation."

When you trust the fact that Jesus Christ died and paid the payment for your sins and rose the third day from the grave you become God's child. When you receive Jesus Christ as your personal Savior you pass from death into life. Whisper a prayer to God. Acknowledge that you sin, that you are not perfect. Agree with God that you cannot live up to God's standard of perfection. Tell God that you are putting your complete trust in Christ, and in him alone, to forgive your sins and give you eternal life. The Bible says, "*Yet to all who received him, to those who believed in his name, he gave the right to become children of God,*" (John 1:12 NIV). To run a race we must first begin the race. Apart from salvation by grace alone, through faith alone, in Christ alone, we cannot enter into the blessings that God has for us.

Also, both pathways include the desire to grow spiritually. The believer who has yet to yield to the prompting of the Holy Spirit to desire godly living, will have no interest in spiritual things. Some would say that anyone who doesn't have a desire to live a holy life isn't really saved. I would disagree for two reasons. First, believers have the ability to quench the working of the Holy Spirit. Our flesh has no desire to serve God, so the people who are quenching the work of the Holy Spirit are left without any internal desire or motivation to continue in their relationship with God. As a result saved individuals may cease to grow spiritually. Until each yields again to the working of the Holy Spirit within, he/she will stay in spiritual infancy.

(Your thoughts, impressions and experiences)

14

CHAPTER ONE
THE LEGALISTIC PARADIGM

"It is quite easy to define legalism, but nearly impossible to detect it in ourselves."

Second, my experience, both personally and in observing others, has validated this truth. There are times in my life when I have ignored the prompting of the Holy Spirit. God never left me during these times. Satan has caused me to doubt if I was really saved. He has whispered in my ear, "You can't be a Christian and do that!" But our salvation is not based upon what we do, but on what we are in Christ. We are children of God by declaration of God (John 1:12). Both the legalism path and grace path start out with the same belief in the saving work of Christ Jesus our Lord. But there they must part company.

What is Legalism?

Since we have used the word "*legalism*" let's define its meaning. Legalism is the effort of man seeking to gain approval or blessings from God. The Galatians were legalists who believed that living the Christian life was a matter of keeping some laws instead of being led by the Spirit. It is quite easy to define legalism, but nearly impossible to detect it in ourselves. I have never met a legalist who admitted being legalistic. Therefore, the test of determining if someone is legalistic is not in what they say, but in what they do. There are some definite evidences of legalism.

1. Putting outward behavior before inward change
The focus of legalism is on the actions of people. As long as people are behaving in the acceptable manner, they are considered spiritual.

(Your thoughts, impressions and experiences)

15

*"Legalism creates a 'don't do this'
list assuming the same authority as inspired
Scripture and eliminating the need for the Holy Spirit."*

If someone has a visible problem that looks like sin, then they are not spiritual. Therefore, the obvious focus of legalism is to require Christians to act right in public, regardless of what is happening in their hearts.

2. **Replacing the leading of the Holy Spirit with the dictates of man**
Legalism adds to the sins mentioned in the Bible by creating new man-made sins. These new sins are activities that someone has determined to be hazardous to our Christian testimony based upon someone's own standard of behavior. Legalism creates a "don't do this" list assuming the same authority as inspired Scripture and eliminating the need for the Holy Spirit to show us thoughts, attitudes or actions displeasing to him.

3. **Trying in our own strength to do what only God can accomplish**
Legalism focuses on the self-control of the individual. "Try harder" becomes the challenge of each sermon. Man-made gimmicks are supposed to help us keep our promises to God. We need never come to the point where we acknowledge we cannot do the will of God and humbly go to God for his power.

4. **Making others live up to God's standard**
Threats of banishment from the church are issued in order to force Christians to obey the rules. It doesn't matter if these laws are God's or their own.

(Your thoughts, impressions and experiences)

"When spirituality is determined on the basis of obedience, then a rebellious heart may be left unnoticed."

The pressure from leadership is considered necessary for the church to glorify God. The fact that God has given leaders to the church is taken as proof that those leaders are to enforce rules that are deemed necessary.

5. Placing obedience before submission to the Holy Spirit

Submission is a change of heart; obedience is a change of behavior. When spirituality is determined on the basis of obedience, then a rebellious heart may be left unnoticed. Later on, this rebellious heart may come to the surface, taking everyone by surprise. Many Christians, who were once active in their local church, will no longer darken the doors of the church because they were never taught submission to the Holy Spirit, only obedience.

6. Loving people conditionally based upon performance or appearance

Appearances mean everything to the legalists because legalism focuses on the outward. The style of clothing worn, the words spoken and the business establishments visited must all conform to someone's definition of appropriate. Love and acceptance are conditioned upon how well individuals live up to someone's standard. The believer's performance is always being evaluated, leaving the individual unsure of his or her position within the church.

Love with a spirit

LISTEN THEN DO

PAUL LAWS IN GRACE

Do NOT judge

(Your thoughts, impressions and experiences)

"When Christians share their personal weakness and failing, a legalistic environment will prompt judgment and condemnation."

learn their way of life —

7. Conforming to the customs of a religious culture rather than the leading of God

A key word in the concept of legalism is "*conforming*." The believer is focused on not doing what others have determined to be worldly, and doing what they have determined to be godly, thereby acting in a seemingly correct manner. Those who conform to the norm of the church are considered godly. Many of those who are, therefore, considered godly have no concept of what it means to be led by God.

8. Focusing on the image of the group, not the needs of the individual.

Christians who are not submitted to the leading of the Holy Spirit often reflect their pain through negative outward behavior. Legalism creates an environment where it is OK to believe hurting people within the church makes the church look bad. Hurting people often act in anger or in distracting ways. Rather than seeking to help the hurting person, a legalistic environment seeks to remove them. There is no mercy or grace in legalism.

9. Dishonesty amongst Sincere Christians

When Christians share their personal weakness and failing, a legalistic environment will prompt judgment and condemnation. The struggling Christian is faced with a dilemma.

(Your thoughts, impressions and experiences)

18

"Since the focus of legalism is only on obedience, Christians never grow further in their love relationship with God."

Should Christians be honest and admit their faults or cover them up and pretend they don't exist? Most often Christians will put on their spiritual mask rather than face the disapproval of their leaders and other church members.

10. Motivated by guilt

Since the focus of legalism is only on obedience, Christians never grow further in their love relationship with God. Without godly love to motivate believers, legalistic leaders must resort to guilt. A legalist will say things like, "After all Christ did for you, you owe it to him to do. . . ." Implied is that spiritual Christians do the things their leaders want, fulfilling an obligation to God.

11. Quantity, not quality ministries

True spiritual growth is a slow, progressive work of God within us. There are no shortcuts to spiritual maturity. Legalism is an attempt to bypass the process of spiritual growth with "spiritual-looking" Christians. To accomplish this appearance legalists must shift their focus to something they can see and count. The criterion for spirituality begins with the words, "How many. . . ."

*   *How many services attended each week?*
*   *How many minutes spent reading the Bible and praying?*
*   *How many people witnessed to during the week?*
*   *How many ministries or positions held?*

Rel with God first

(Your thoughts, impressions and experiences)

"Legalism seeks to immediately correct all the wrongs rather than allow God time to work in the hearts of people."

Legalistic leaders are not exempt themselves from the tyranny of the " how many?"

* How many services on Sunday morning?
* How many attend church Sunday night?
* How many came forward or were baptized?
* How many degrees mounted on the wall?

12. Lip service to the Holy Spirit

Since there are so many passages of Scripture that state the Holy Spirit to be the power of God who leads us and enables us to live godly lives, the legalist must agree with Scripture. Because of this agreement with Scripture, legalists don't think they are legalistic. However, they are giving only lip service to the Holy Spirit. You will not hear the legalist say, "Go home and pray over this decision and do what you feel the Holy Spirit is telling you to do." Instead of directing people to the Holy Spirit, legalists play Holy Spirit, telling other Christians how to live their lives.

13. Dwelling on the negative

Legalism focuses on determining what issues or conducts are unacceptable and then creates rules to avoid the unacceptable and fix what is wrong in other Christians' lives. Legalism seeks to immediately correct all the wrongs rather than allow God time to work in the hearts of people. This philosophy leads to a crusading attitude against real or perceived evil.

(Your thoughts, impressions and experiences)

20

CHAPTER ONE
THE LEGALISTIC PARADIGM

"God is trying to bring us to the point of brokenness so that we will turn to him to live the Christian life the correct way."

If a legalistic organization has a publication, the primary articles will deal with people, organizations or social trends they oppose. Sermons are negative under the auspices of preaching against sin. Members of the congregation live in fear lest they be next on the hit list. Disagreeing with the leadership is the quickest way of making the list and becoming part of "the evil."

The left side of the chart on page 12 presents the path of legalism. Legalism is rooted in pride because it is based upon our natural desire to do God's work ourselves.

We want to be spiritual, so we will do the things that will make us spiritual. We want to live the Christian life rather than allow God to live the Christian life within us.

When we are dependent upon ourselves, then we must draw upon our own strength. This "energy of the flesh" may last for a while, but it is no substitute for God's power. Those with greater will power can last longer, but in the end our efforts just can't give us what we desire, the blessings of God.

I have heard (and preached, sad to say) messages on growing in love, which is good, but then heard the power of the message diminished by the words, "Now let's go out there and try harder to be more loving." Then when we fail, and fail we must, we feel even more guilty for not doing what we know we should do.

(Your thoughts, impressions and experiences)

"Where legalism is based upon pride, grace is based upon humility."

God knows we will try and fail at living the Christian life, so he has given us his Holy Spirit to show us the error of our ways. This is good! The way the Holy Spirit does this correcting is through trials and tribulations in our life. That is not so good! But it really is good! God is trying to bring us to the point of brokenness so that we will turn to him to live the Christian life the correct way.

Often our pride will not allow us to be broken through the trial and tribulation process. There are some other options. We can come to the conclusion that we have been weak and need to be stronger. So we try harder! Trouble is, that puts us right back at the top of the legalistic path, trying harder to live for God through our own efforts. This has become a life-long vicious circle for some Christians.

Another option for the legalistic Christian is to just quit. Their motto is "Christianity didn't work for me!" I know far too many of these individuals. They have become disheartened and discouraged by their failure to live the Christian life. By all outward appearances they seemed to be strong Christians, but inwardly they know they are failures. One day they threw in the towel and gave up on the Christian life. Their desire to grow spiritually is destroyed by failure. They were truly saved, but the path they were shown couldn't produce true godliness. I don't blame them; I feel sorry for them. I blame those who led them down the road to ruin. But then I feel sorry for these blind leaders because they are just repeating lessons learned from other teachers.

(Your thoughts, impressions and experiences)

"When we come humbly to God acknowledging our weakness and seeking his power, the Holy Spirit is freed to go to work on our behalf."

In contrast to the "breaking" path is the "blessing" path on the right depicting the road to true spiritual growth. Where legalism is based upon pride, grace is based upon humility. Twice in the New Testament we are told *"God resists the proud and gives grace to the humble"* (1 Peter 5:5; James 4:6). Humility admits "I can not do it. I can not live the Christian life by myself. I am helpless and hopeless apart from God." Does that sound severe? It is! But this truth is the very foundation upon which the Christian life is built.

Until we come to the point in our walk with God where we acknowledge our helplessness, we continue to try to help ourselves. Self-sufficiency didn't work for our salvation and it will not work for our Christian growth.

Once in humility, we come to the point of total dependence on God's grace, we begin to rely upon the power of God to bring us to spiritual maturity. We are never told in God's Word that we must muster up the power to live for God. We are told to trust God, not try harder. God's power is the only power big enough to overcome the opposition of Satan. God's power is only given to us when we are weak and broken, willing to submit to God's will in our lives (2 Corinthians 12:9-10).

When we come humbly to God acknowledging our weakness and seeking his power, the Holy Spirit is freed to go to work on our behalf. If you learn only one truth in this book, I pray it will be that all we desire from the Christian life is a product of the Holy Spirit working within us.

(Your thoughts, impressions and experiences)

"When we understand God's grace our understanding produces God's joy."

_____

_____

_____

_____

_____

_____

_____

_____

_____

(Your thoughts, impressions and experiences)

When we are yielded to the Holy Spirit we will celebrate victory over sin. We will experience the fruit of the Spirit operating within us. We will enjoy an intimate relationship with God filling our hearts with love for him and for others. There is a danger. We can begin on the blessing path of living by grace but be seduced to cross over to the breaking path. It happened to the believers at the Galatian church (Galatians 5:4). We can become proud of our spiritual growth that was accomplished by the Holy Spirit. Pride will always move us immediately to the breaking path. Then we find that we need our pride to be broken again before God can continue to mold us by his grace. I pray you will find this book useful as you listen to the Holy Spirit's direction for your spiritual growth. When we understand God's grace our understanding produces God's joy. I wish you joy!

FOUR CORNERSTONES

MORE GRACE	**KNOW THE ENEMY WITHIN**
TRUSTING GOD FOR GODLINESS	**HUMILITY**

CHAPTER ONE
QUESTIONS AND DISCUSSION

Are you ready to acknowledge to God, and yourself, your inability to live the Christian life? God wants to live his life in and through you, but you must step aside and allow him to give you the power. Spend some time in prayer, humbling yourself before God and allowing the Holy Spirit to direct your thoughts toward him.

QUESTIONS AND DISCUSSION:

1. When you die do you know for certain where you will spend all of eternity and why?

    _____

    _____

    _____

    _____

2. Study the chart on page 12 and evaluate your Christian experience. On which side of the chart would you place yourself? Why?

    _____

    _____

    _____

    _____

3. Define legalism.

    _____

    _____

4. Which of the evidences of legalism have you seen in yourself?

_____

_____

_____

_____

_____

5. Why is legalism a great hindrance to true spirituality?

_____

_____

_____

_____

_____

PROJECT:

Meditate on the contents of this chapter. Ask God to reveal to you where legalism has tainted your understanding of the Christian life. Confess these as sins (missing the true mark) and turn from them.

_____

_____

_____

_____

_____

_____

CHAPTER TWO
NOW WHAT? MORE GRACE!

"The relationship we began at the time of salvation is only the beginning. Now God wants that relationship to deepen and grow."

When we received Christ as our Savior, we received God's greatest gift. We began the great adventure of following Jesus Christ. We also began a relationship with Jesus. All of our sins - past, present and future - are now forgiven. God calls us his children and he is our Father. Nothing can ever change that! God will never go back on his word. Eternal life is ours right now and heaven will be ours for all of eternity.

But what we may not realize is that although salvation is God's greatest gift, it is not his only gift for us. God has a whole warehouse of gifts for the taking. The relationship we began at the time of salvation is only the beginning. Now God wants that relationship to deepen and grow. As we progress in our spiritual journey, God grants us many gifts along the way. All gifts come to us by the grace of God, and all are received by faith.

The purpose of this book is to aid us in this spiritual growth so we can discover more of God's gifts. Each lesson takes us a step further into the forest of God's blessings. The journey is fraught with hazards and many fall by the wayside. Satan wants to hinder us, and even some well-meaning Christians might add to the confusion. However, with the light of God's Word illuminating the path before us, we can make progress.

So, let us begin at the beginning. But where is the beginning? I have more than fifty books in my personal library that present various plans on how to grow in spiritual maturity.

(Your thoughts, impressions and experiences)

"The beginning point [of the Christian life] has to be God himself."

_____

_____

_____

_____

_____

_____

_____

_____

_____

_____

_____

_____

_____

_____

_____

(Your thoughts, impressions and experiences)

Some begin with obedience to God as the first step in Christian growth. (I hope by the time you are through with this series you will know why that cannot possibly be the starting point.) Another author begins with confession, another with worship. They each have their reasons, why their method or way is the logical starting point for a deeper life or relationship with God.

But the beginning point of the Christian life is not in us or anything we do, any more than salvation begins with us. The beginning point has to be God himself. Listen to the Word of God and allow the Holy Spirit to speak to you.

"Being confident of this very thing, that <u>he</u> who hath begun a good work in you <u>will perform it</u> until the day of Jesus Christ."
(Philippians 1:6)

All work of a spiritual nature is the work of God. Our salvation was the beginning of that good work within us. Salvation is the starting point of our spiritual life. Having begun our spiritual pilgrimage, God will be the One to bring it to completion. The day of Jesus Christ is the day we stand before him in heaven. So everything of a spiritual nature, sandwiched in between our salvation and our going to heaven, is also a work of God!

"For I know that <u>in me</u> (that is, in my flesh,) <u>dwelleth no good thing</u>; for to will is present with me, but how to perform that which is good I find not."
(Romans 7:18)

CHAPTER TWO
NOW WHAT? MORE GRACE!

"Everything we do, apart from God's enabling power, is an act of the flesh."

This verse is the personal testimony of one of the greatest Christians who ever lived, the apostle Paul. Paul says by the inspiration of the Holy Spirit, that our flesh cannot accomplish spiritual good. Everything we do, apart from God's enabling power, is an act of the flesh. As we will see in more depth in future lessons, one of the first things we must come to acknowledge is that our flesh can't do anything to please or serve God. As long as we live according to the flesh, we will not be able to enjoy God's blessings.

Contrary to popular belief, willpower does not solve all of life's problems. In fact, personal willpower can hinder our spiritual growth. Where there is a "personal will," there is no "way" for the Holy Spirit to work within us.

"For it is God who worketh in you both to will and to do of his good pleasure."
(Philippians 2:13)

The word "will" is the word that means to desire or wish. The desire to obey God comes from God. When we get to section two, "The Seven Elements of Spiritual Growth," we'll see how we can either hinder God or surrender to his putting the desire to obey him within us. The point we want to see here is that the desire and the power to obey God comes from God, and is a part of his work within us.

"For the grace of God that bringeth salvation hath appeared to all men, teaching us that, denying ungodliness and worldly lusts, we should live soberly, righteously and godly in this present age."
(Titus 2:11-12)

(Your thoughts, impressions and experiences)

*"Once works are added to
grace, then grace ceases to be grace."*

The same grace that saved us is going to teach us how to live in a manner that is pleasing to God. No list of rules or laws can produce the ability to live for God. In fact, rules often have the opposite effect. When I see a sign saying, "Do not touch," I feel the urge to touch. If I had never seen the sign, it probably would not have entered my mind to touch the forbidden object. Laws or rules are not the way to Christian growth. Grace is!

Grace is one of those words Christians use a lot, but many do not understand its meaning. Grace is an unmerited, undeserved, and unearned gift that incurs no debt or obligation. The Bible contrasts grace with works. Works refer to actions we do to earn or become deserving of something. Grace is something we are given out of God's unconditional love for us.

Grace and works, like oil and water, do not mix. The apostle Paul wrote the Roman believers,

*"And if by grace,
it is no longer by works; if it were, grace
would no longer be grace"*
(Romans 11:6 NIV).

Works played no active part in our salvation. We are saved *"by grace through faith"* (Ephesians 2:8). Salvation is not a combination of our good works and God's grace. Once works are added to grace, then grace ceases to be grace.

It is important to note also that a grace gift incurs no debt or obligation.

(Your thoughts, impressions and experiences)

CHAPTER TWO
NOW WHAT? MORE GRACE!

"Having faith is not a work on our part. Faith is a response to God reaching out to us and touching us with his grace."

Let us imagine, for a moment, that someone gives you $1,000. As they give you this gift they say, "This is a gift, it has nothing to do with what you have done in the past or will do in the future. I am giving you this because I love you and I want you to have it." That would be a grace gift.

However, let's say that same person later gives you a call and says, "You know that $1,000 I gave you? Well, now I expect you to be at my house every Saturday to mow my lawn." What has happened? Their gift is no longer a grace gift, but really wages paid in advance for mowing their lawn. Grace ceases to be grace when it is mixed with works.

The same is true with God. God saves us by his grace. That means there is no debt or obligation placed upon us to do something for God. We do not owe God anything in return. If we owed God, then our salvation was just a prepayment for works that God wanted us to do for him. That would make our salvation a reward for our works instead of a gift of God's grace.

In Ephesians 2:8-9 we read we are saved "*by grace through faith.*" Before we were saved by God's grace, we searched for answers to fill the void in our lives. While we were seeking to fill this void we found God's grace and faith in his Son. We responded to the offer of God's grace with faith. Having faith is not a work on our part. Faith is a response to God reaching out to us and touching us with his grace. Faith is not a "work," or then we are saved by works.

(Your thoughts, impressions and experiences)

"God's Word works in those who believe (trust) God."

Faith is the only authorized response to grace. As we grow in our relationship with God, He is going to ask us to believe him for even more blessings. Faith is believing God. Faith is also an act of the will, not of the intellect or emotions. All of this will be explained in depth in future chapters. For now let's just remember that God, by his grace, is going to continue to do the work he began in us at the moment of our salvation.

Much of what we are going to be studying in these chapters will deal with our responsibility in our faith responses to God. I don't have "5,000 Easy Steps to Spirituality." I don't even have twelve steps. Much of what God wants us to do is simply to believe him.

*"For this cause also thank
we God without ceasing, because,
when ye received the word of
God which ye heard of us, ye received
it not as the word of men, but as it is in
truth, the word of God,
which effectually worketh also
in you that believe"*
(1 Thessalonians 2:13).

God's Word works in those who believe (trust) God.

We are great for getting the cart before the horse; we always have been. When Jesus lived on earth, there was a group of religious people called Pharisees. This group had thousands of rules to live by and thought by keeping all the rules, they were truly spiritual. However, despite all their religious attitudes and rules, they did not believe Jesus.

(Your thoughts, impressions and experiences)

CHAPTER TWO
NOW WHAT? MORE GRACE!

"Faith is the only authorized response to grace."

*J*esus called them whitewashed tombs. The Pharisees were pretty on the outside but full of maggots and worms on the inside. They were full of doing but empty of believing. Religious people, they were obedient to the law of God, but with hearts far from him.

The purpose of this book is to steer far from the empty religion of forced obedience to God, to a place where God is changing us from the inside out. When the inside is right, the outside will follow suit.

WHERE ARE WE GOING?

On a wall in our home is a map of Hawaii. On the coffee table are some brochures with pictures of palm trees and sandy beaches. You may have guessed there is a trip to Hawaii in store for us this winter. But before I go I want to know where we are going and what it will be like when we get there.

Likewise, I thought it might be exciting for you to see where we are going with these lessons. What will it be like when we get there? What are some of these other gifts that God will start producing in our lives as we grow in our relationship with him? Here are just a few:

1. **A loving, exciting and satisfying relationship with God**
   I am not talking about some sterile, intellectual knowledge *about* God. I am talking about an intimate, warm, experiential relationship *with* God.

(Your thoughts, impressions and experiences)

33

"Nothing on earth compares to intimacy with God."

This relationship is a love relationship that is just as real and satisfying as any human one. Talking with God and feeling his love can be the greatest experience of your life. King David put it this way,

> *"As the deer pants*
> *for streams of water,*
> *so my soul pants for you,*
> *O God. My soul thirsts for*
> *God, for the living God.*
> *When can I go and*
> *meet with God?"*
> (Psalm 42:1-2 NIV).

Being with God becomes the highlight of the day. Nothing on earth compares to intimacy with God, just you and the Almighty God of heaven and earth spending time together. Nothing you have ever experienced can match this unique relationship with God.

2. **The power of God in your life**
   The apostle Paul describes the greatness of this power:

> *"Now unto him who is able to do exceedingly abundantly above all that we ask or think . . . according to the power that worketh in us"*
> (Ephesians 3:20).

Notice the piling on of superlatives, power to achieve "*exceedingly . . . abundantly . . . above all . . . that we can ask . . . or think.*" Friend, that is power, power available to us!

(Your thoughts, impressions and experiences)

"God does not hand these out as rewards to those who have been good. They are gifts of God's grace, received by faith."

"Earlier in this same epistle Paul prayed for all believers that they might know. . .

"What is the exceeding greatness of his power <u>toward us who believe</u>, according to the working of his mighty power"
(Ephesians 1:19).

To those who continue to believe God, he gives a tremendous power. This power will enable us to have great victories in our lives and allow him to do great things for us.

3. **Filled with "the fruit of the Spirit"**
The fruit of the Spirit is listed in Galatians 5:22-23,

"But the fruit of the Spirit is love, joy, peace, longsuffering, gentleness, goodness, faith, meekness, self-control."
(Galatians 5:22-23)

These virtues are more gifts from God. Take a minute and meditate on each one. Imagine what it would be like to have each "fruit" dominating your life and relationships.

God does not hand these out as rewards to those who have been good. They are gifts of God's grace, received by faith,

"Now may the God of hope fill you with all <u>joy and peace in believing</u>, that ye may abound in hope, <u>through the power of the Holy Spirit</u>"
(Romans 15:13).

(Your thoughts, impressions and experiences)

35

"There is no victory over sin in the energy of the flesh, only in the power of the Holy Spirit."

4. **Victory over Sin**

Every one of us has temptations that continue to plague us. We may have to fight temptations every day of our life. However, we do have power over sin.

This I say then, walk in the Spirit and ye shall not fulfill the lust of the flesh."
(Galatians 5:16).

There is no victory over sin in the energy of the flesh, only in the power of the Holy Spirit.

When God is in control of our lives, we have victory over sin.

"There hath no temptation taken you but such as is common to man; but God is faithful, who will not allow you to be tempted above that ye are able, but will, with the temptation, also make the way to escape, that ye may be able to bear it"
(1 Corinthians 10:13).

Without God's way of escape there is no victory over sin.

5. **Being led and directed by the Holy Spirit**

God wants to lead every believer in every decision in life.

"For as many as are led by the Spirit of God, they are the sons of God"
(Romans 8:14).

(Your thoughts, impressions and experiences)

"Whatever God calls me to do for him, I want it to be a successful effort."

God has a perfect will and plan for us. This plan is another of God's grace gifts reserved for us. Revealing this plan for us is the work of the Holy Spirit, who lives within each believer.

"But as it is written,
eye hath not seen,
nor ear heard,
neither have entered
into the heart of man,
the things which God hath
prepared for them
that love him.
But God hath
revealed them unto us
by his Spirit;
for the Spirit searcheth all things,
yea, the deep things of God"
(1 Corinthians 2:9-10).

Christians cannot afford to be without this gift of God, which gives us the right decision for every situation in life. In fact, as the Holy Spirit reveals God's perfect plan for our lives, we discover our true purpose in life.

6. Fruitful service
The word "fruitful" means successful, not successful from man's point of view, but successful according to God's definition.

For some believers it might mean winning hundreds of people to the Lord. For others it might mean helping believers grow in their newfound faith. For every believer, though, it means being a member of God's winning team.

(Your thoughts, impressions and experiences)

37

"God has already shown the depths of his forgiveness in forgiving us all our sins. So, another one of his grace gifts is forgiveness which enables us to forgive those who have hurt us."

Nothing is more frustrating than failing. I worked as a commission salesman for three months. I never sold anything and never made a cent. I never want to do that again! Whatever God calls me to do for him, I want it to be a successful effort.

Jesus said,

> *"A tree is known by its fruit"*
> (Matthew 12:33).

In other words, by our fruit, or lack of fruit, people will know about our relationship with God. I want a successful ministry that reflects God working in me to produce good fruit. As believers are enlightened by the Holy Spirit and fulfill the roles God has chosen for them, they become successful members of his team.

7. **Ability to forgive**
Alexander Pope said, "To err is human, to forgive divine." Our problem is that we aren't divine. However, as we grow in our relationship with God, we become more like Christ. Where once we held bitterness and resentment, God fills us with his forgiveness.

Only then are we able to obey the Biblical admonition,

> *"And be ye kind one to another, tenderhearted, forgiving one another, even as God, for Christ's sake, hath forgiven you"*
> (Ephesians 4:32).

(Your thoughts, impressions and experiences)

CHAPTER TWO
NOW WHAT? MORE GRACE!

"Many Christians have never enjoyed any of the blessings God eagerly wants to pour out upon them right now."

God has already shown the depths of his forgiveness in forgiving us all our sins. So, another one of his grace gifts is forgiveness which enables us to forgive those who have hurt us.

These are only a few of the gifts that God will start producing in our lives as our relationship with him grows. His grace is a continuous free gift to those who receive it into their lives.

DECISION TIME

Now I have some good news and some bad news for you. The bad news first: You can live out the rest of your life never experiencing any of the rest of God's gifts. Sad to say, this is true for many Christians. Assured of salvation and a place in heaven someday, many Christians have never enjoyed any of the blessings God eagerly wants to pour out upon them right now. These Christians live defeated and powerless lives, having never sought the rest of God's blessings.

Some Christians might say, "I can't change. I am the way I am, and I will always be this way," denying the supernatural power of God to transform them. Other Christians may say, "I want to grow as a Christian, so I will try harder to be more spiritual." They also deny the supernatural power of God to transform them. Trying harder is not the answer.

(Your thoughts, impressions and experiences)

"We don't have to live a defeated Christian life.'

_____

_____

_____

_____

_____

_____

_____

_____

_____

_____

_____

_____

_____

_____

(Your thoughts, impressions and experiences)

Study the chart on page 12 of the introduction. This chart reflects the desire most Christians feel to grow in their relationship with God. The more difficult path to follow travels through the Legalistic Breaking Path towards brokenness, a willingness to depend upon God's grace and the interaction of the Holy Spirit working through us rather than on us. Note that humility will always lead us through this path to true understanding and fulfillment.

Now the good news: We don't have to live a defeated Christian life. We can choose to continue to grow by faith in our relationship with God. The choice is ours. The rest of these lessons will give us the understanding of how this growth is going to take place, laying out in detail the seven elements necessary for spiritual growth. We will also see the place prayer, the church and suffering play in equipping us to grow. I pray that you will come along on our journey into God's warehouse of grace gifts.

If you want to grow in your relationship with God, may I suggest a prayer to him? In this prayer express your desire to grow in your relationship with Christ. Admit your inability to make yourself grow spiritually. Tell God that you are totally dependent upon him. Ask God for the continued desire and power to finish each chapter. Then in true humility depend upon God for his grace.

CHAPTER TWO
QUESTIONS AND DISCUSSION

1. Read Hebrews 10:14.
   A. How do we appear in God's eyes?

   _Bee _____

   _____

   _____

   _____

   _____

   B. How long will we appear that way?

   _____

   _____

   _____

   _____

2. Read John 3:16 and Romans 8:38-39. Our salvation is a gift of God's unconditional love. That gift is said to be everlasting.
   A. Can an "everlasting gift" not last forever?

   _____

   _____

   _____

   _____

   _____

B. How does knowing there is nothing that can ever come between us and God's love for us, produce security within us?

_____

_____

_____

_____

_____

3. Read Ephesians 2:8-9 and Colossians 2:6. If we are saved "by grace through faith," then how do we live the Christian life?

faith is take him as he used

_____

_____

_____

4. Look at the list of seven grace gifts in the "Where are we going?" section beginning on page 33.
   A. Which ones are most important to you?

God has a plan for me,

a life able to get you to him a

praise God.

   B. Why?

_____

_____

CHAPTER THREE
GETTING TO KNOW THE ENEMY WITHIN

*"Paul had the battle. I have the battle.
You have the battle, the battle of the flesh vs. the Spirit."*

In chapter one we saw seven exciting grace gifts. In the questions and discussion section you were asked to pick the ones most important to you. Keep these in mind as you continue in these lessons. These grace gifts will be your motivators, keeping you going when the going gets tough, and it will get tough.

In this chapter we are going to focus on a great battle. It is going on inside us every minute of every day. Romans 7:18-25 lays out the battle for us.

*"For I know
that in me, that is, in my <u>flesh</u>,
dwelleth no good thing: for to will is
present with me, but to do that
which is good (is) not. For the good
which I would do I do not: but the
evil which I would not, that I practice.
But if what I would not, that I do, it is no
more I that do it, but sin which dwelleth
in me. I find then the law, that,
to me who would do good, evil is
present. For I delight in the law of
God after the inward man: but I see
a different law in my members, warring
against the law of my mind, and
bringing me into captivity under the
law of sin which is in my members.
Wretched man that I am! who shall
deliver me out of the body of this
death? I thank God through Jesus
Christ our Lord. So then I of myself
with the mind, indeed, serve the
law of God; but with
the <u>flesh</u> the law of sin"*
Romans 7:18-25 (ASV).

(Your thoughts, impressions and experiences)

"The enemy is the flesh and, if we are going to have the victory, we need to be able to identify and understand the enemy."

Paul had the battle. I have the battle. You have the battle, the battle of the flesh vs. the Spirit. How important is this battle? A major consequence of losing this battle is,

"That you do not do what you want"
(Galatians 5:17 NIV).

The enemy is the flesh and, if we are going to have the victory, we need to be able to identify and understand the enemy. When the Bible uses the word "flesh" in this context, it is not referring to physical flesh. Rather, God is speaking of the old patterns, desires and habits by which we have attempted to get all our needs supplied in the past. Instead of seeking Christ and trusting Him to meet our needs, we revert to these old thoughts, attitudes and actions called "the flesh." We can classify these old habits into three categories: dirty rotten flesh, I did it my way flesh, and counterfeit godliness flesh. All three of these different faces of the flesh are the enemy. All three will keep us from obtaining the rest of God's grace gifts.

DIRTY ROTTEN FLESH

In Galatians 5:19-21 we have a partial list of the works of dirty rotten flesh,

"Now the works of the flesh are evident, which are: adultery, fornication, uncleanness, lewdness, idolatry, sorcery, hatred, contentions, jealousies, outbursts of wrath, selfish ambitions, dissensions, heresies, envy, murders, drunkenness, revelries, and the like. . ."
Galatians 5:19-21 (NKJV).

(Your thoughts, impressions and experiences)

44

*" 'I did it my way' flesh does not
actively fight the Holy Spirit. It ignores Him."*

These actions are all flagrant violations of the Word of God. The Christians who commit such acts usually know they are wrong and suffer from a burden of guilt.

These are the Christian adulterers, spouse abusers or child molesters. They have violent tempers. They cheat on their income tax or steal from their employers.

These Christians are the hypocrites in the church that the world is always talking about. They are also the excuses the unsaved use for rejecting Christ. It is obvious to everyone that the flesh is in control of his or her life. Dirty rotten flesh actively fights against the Holy Spirit in believers.

I DID IT MY WAY FLESH

Not so obvious but nonetheless fleshly, this flesh does not actively fight the Holy Spirit. "I did it my way" flesh ignores him. This flesh shows itself in Christians who leave God out of great portions of their lives. These are Christians who don't pray, don't read God's Word and don't serve God, living their lives for self.

We know that Noah lived in the midst of great wickedness. Describing man's evil we read,

"And God saw that the wickedness of man was great on the earth, and that every imagination of the thoughts of his heart was only evil continually"
(Genesis 6:5).

(Your thoughts, impressions and experiences)

"The evil is in what is absent."

It is easy to imagine the murders, rapes and pillage that might have occurred.

But, Jesus gave us another insight into the evil surrounding Noah,

"And as it was in the days of Noah,
so shall it be also in the days
of the Son of man.
They did eat, they drank,
they married wives, they were
given in marriage,
until the day that Noah
entered into the ark, and the flood
came, and destroyed them all"
(Luke 17:26-27 NKJV).

Where is the great evil here? They ate, they drank (it doesn't say they got drunk), they got engaged and married. These are common everyday activities, so why are they said to be evil? The evil is in what is absent. Man, in Noah's time, left God completely out of the picture.

The "I did it my way" Christians are guilty of the same evil, going about their everyday lives ignoring God. Being saved and not guilty of any of the "big, bad" sins, these Christians feel they are doing pretty well. Since they compare their flesh with the "dirty rotten" flesh, they feel they are doing just fine.

The apostle Paul said that as we get closer to the return of Christ, we will have more "I did it my way" Christians,

" . . . lovers of pleasure more than
lovers of God; having a form of godli-
ness, but denying the power . . . "
(2 Timothy 3:4-5).

(Your thoughts, impressions and experiences)

46

"The 'I did it my way' flesh is just as much an enemy of the Spirit as the 'dirty rotten' flesh."

There are many Christians who love the world more than they love God. The way these Christians spend their time speaks volumes concerning their lack of interest in spiritual things.

The "I did it my way" flesh is just as much an enemy of the Spirit as the "dirty rotten" flesh. Ignoring God will keep us from his grace gifts and prevent us from growing in our relationship with God.

COUNTERFEIT GODLINESS FLESH

"Dirty rotten" flesh fights the Holy Spirit and "I did it my way" flesh ignores the Holy Spirit. "Counterfeit godliness" flesh impersonates the Holy Spirit. This looks and seems like the real thing, but it is not.

The Christians with "counterfeit godliness" flesh are active in church. These Christians may teach Sunday school, work in AWANA, sing in the choir and in general are there every time the doors of the church are open. The problem is not in what they do but in why they do it.

This type of flesh seeks to gain the praise and admiration of others by doing something religious. These Christians aren't doing it for God; they are doing it for self. Perhaps some like the warm, fuzzy feeling they get when they are at church. Others may like the attention and admiration of other Christians as they perform. But whatever the motivation, it is not pleasing to God because it is of the flesh.

(Your thoughts, impressions and experiences)

47

"Many Christians are trying to do the work of the Lord in the energy of the flesh."

Along with fleshly motivation is fleshly energy. Many Christians are trying to do the work of the Lord in the energy of the flesh. Veiled in a counterfeit godliness and power, they go about trying to serve God. For a while they might seem successful, but sooner or later problems will arise. Christian "burnout" is evidence of trying to do the work of the Lord in the energy of the flesh. God's power is endless. Ours isn't.

In my years of ministry I have seen scores of pastors, missionaries and laypeople drop by the wayside. Perhaps these burned out Christians didn't get their way on some issue, or they didn't receive credit for a successful project. Or, perhaps they just ran out of strength. Whatever the symptom, the root problem is usually that the flesh has taken control. These Christians have traded Spirit-controlled power for a powerless, fleshly religion.

The apostle Paul knew both sides of that street. Concerning his religious days he reflected,

"Though I myself have reasons
for such confidence.
If anyone else
thinks he has reasons to put
confidence in the flesh, I have more:
circumcised on the eighth day,
of the people of Israel, of the tribe of
Benjamin, a Hebrew of Hebrews; in
regard to the law, a Pharisee; as for
zeal, persecuting the church; as for
legalistic righteousness, faultless"
(Philippians 3:4-6 NIV).

(Your thoughts, impressions and experiences)

48

"Not only is counterfeit godliness inferior, but it also hinders us from growing in spiritual maturity and receiving God's other grace gifts"

In all outward appearances before Jesus revealed himself, Paul had a relationship with God. In reality all Paul had was an empty religion. Paul came to understand the emptiness of religion one day and looking back said,

"But whatever was to my profit, I now consider loss for the sake of Christ; What is more, I consider everything a loss compared to the surpassing greatness of knowing Christ Jesus my Lord, for whose sake I have lost all things. I consider them rubbish, that I may gain Christ" (Philippians 3:7-8 NIV).

Paul traded in his empty religion for an intimate relationship with God. In comparison the religion was garbage; the relationship was true gain. Sad to say, there are many Christians who appear to have a close relationship with God, but in reality have only a fleshly religion. Counterfeit godliness, produced by the flesh, is a poor substitute for the real thing. Not only is counterfeit godliness inferior, but it also hinders us from growing in spiritual maturity and receiving God's other grace gifts.

All Flesh Is the Enemy of God

It doesn't matter what type of flesh it has, the flesh will fight the working of the Holy Spirit within us,

"For the flesh lusts against the spirit, and the spirit against the flesh; and these are contrary to one another" (Galatians 5:17 NKJV).

(Your thoughts, impressions and experiences)

49

"The 'I did it my way' flesh, in ignoring God, keeps the believer away from the Word, thus eliminating one of the essential elements needed for spiritual growth."

This is not just the "dirty rotten" flesh, but the "I did it my way" and "counterfeit godliness" types of flesh, too. All three forms are the enemy of the Holy Spirit.

Each type of flesh seeks to defeat the Holy Spirit by taking advantage of our self-centered nature. The dirty rotten flesh is the most obvious. We want what we want, and nobody is going to keep us from getting it. Our materialistic society today encourages this flesh. "If it feels good, do it!" has become the motto of the masses. While the Holy Spirit is seeking to develop unconditional love for others, the flesh is reinforcing the love of self with which we are all born.

"I did it my way" flesh feeds on our pride, too. Satan uses this flesh to keep the Holy Spirit from becoming involved in the process of our spiritual growth. We are not going to grow spiritually by osmosis. Two ingredients are necessary for spiritual growth to occur, the Word of God and the Holy Spirit. The Holy Spirit of God uses the Holy Word of God to produce the holy child of God.

The "I did it my way" flesh, in ignoring God, keeps the believer away from the Word, thus eliminating one of the essential elements needed for spiritual growth. Also, God gave us the Holy Spirit to guide and teach us, but he can't do that if we are ignoring him.

The "counterfeit godliness" flesh is effective against the Holy Spirit because it is so hard to detect. The most dangerous counterfeit is the one that most closely resembles the real thing.

(Your thoughts, impressions and experiences)

50

"Satan will use any means at his disposal to keep us from enjoying the fullness of God's blessings."

Through legalism and outward pressure, congregations have been misled into thinking they are godly, when in fact they are victims of counterfeit godliness.

Satan will use any means at his disposal to keep us from enjoying the fullness of God's blessings. Remember that Satan is a liar (John 8:44). The Devil will tell us that a little sin in our lives won't really hurt us. This is a lie! If "the father of lies" can't get us on this lie, then he will tell us that we don't need to be in the Word of God regularly. This, too, is a lie. If we see through this lie, then the Evil One will encourage us to do something for God, but in our own wisdom and energy. We must see this lie as another of Satan's strategies and a part of our spiritual warfare.

Defeating the Flesh

Identifying the enemy within is half the battle. Now that we are aware of the three faces of the flesh, we can be looking for their symptoms. This awareness will improve our reaction time, the time it takes for us to realize the flesh is controlling us. When our "dirty rotten flesh" tempts us to lie or cheat we can recognize it and say, "That is of the flesh and is an enemy of God. I refuse to let this sin rob me of God's grace gifts."

To defeat "I did it my way" flesh, we can be proactive rather than just reactive. Each morning we can get up and say, "I am not going to have an 'I did it my way' flesh day. I want all God's grace gifts today. I need them all today!"

(Your thoughts, impressions and experiences)

"When it comes to the issues of the flesh, we have one clear admonition —FLEE IT!"

Then we can get into the Word of God and allow the Holy Spirit to lead and direct us.

For those Christians who are involved in Christian service, there is the need for periodic evaluation. Why am I doing this ministry? Am I involved in ministry for my glory or for God's? Am I performing in my fleshly energy or am I relying on God's power to do the job? Am I letting God direct me or am I trying to figure out in my own mind what to do? Being aware of "counterfeit godliness" flesh can motivate us to change, avoid burnout and worse, God's discipline.

When it comes to the issues of the flesh, we have one clear admonition — FLEE IT!

"But you,
O man of God,
flee from
all of this,
(foolish and harmful desires)"
(1 Timothy 6:11 NIV).

"Wherefore,
my dearly beloved,
flee from
idolatry"
(1 Corinthians 10:14).

"Flee from sexual immorality"
(1 Corinthians 6:18 NIV).

"Flee also youthful lusts"
(2 Timothy 2:22 NKJV).

(Your thoughts, impressions and experiences)

CHAPTER THREE
GETTING TO KNOW THE ENEMY WITHIN

"How important is it that we have victory over the flesh?"

When Potiphar's wife tried to seduce him, Joseph didn't stay around to try to reason with her. The Bible says,

"And she caught him by his garment, saying, Lie with me: and he left his garment in her hand, and fled, and got out" (Genesis 39:12).

Joseph had already decided He was not going to give in to the lusts of the flesh. Therefore, when the time came to act, there was no hesitation. Joseph already knew what he wanted to do, so he just did it.

DECISION TIME

How important is it that we have victory over the flesh? Remember the seven grace gifts mentioned in chapter one? Remember which gifts you picked as most important to you? How important is it that these graces become a reality in your life? If they really are important, then victory over the flesh is essential.

Don't worry about the power to achieve victory. You don't have that kind of power. However, God does! The question now is, "do you see the importance of the victory?" Will you believe God's Word? Will you allow God to fill you with the desire and power to be victorious over the flesh? Tell God you want victory over the flesh. Ask him for the continued desire and power to have that victory. Then, review this chapter periodically to remind yourself that all aspects of the undisciplined flesh, that is, not fully submitted to the working of the Holy Spirit, are fully evil.

(Your thoughts, impressions and experiences)

CHAPTER THREE
QUESTIONS AND DISCUSSION

1. Read Romans 8:8.
   A. What other reason do we have for defeating the flesh?

   _____

   _____

   _____

   _____

   B. How important is this victory for you?

   _____

   _____

   _____

   _____

2. What evidence of the three types of flesh mentioned in this chapter have you seen in your own life?

   _____

   _____

   _____

   _____

3. Which type of flesh is your greatest battle?

   _____

   _____

   _____

4. Take a few minutes and list in your journal symptoms of "flesh control" in your life. As you identify them, acknowledge they are hindering you from growing in your relationship with God, from receiving God's grace gifts in your life and from being effective in your service to God.

_____

_____

_____

_____

5. If there are any fleshly activities in your life that you have not already decided to flee, do so now.

_____

_____

_____

_____

6. Each day ask God to help you identify activities of the flesh at the time of temptation.

_____

_____

_____

7. Each day ask God to give you the power to withstand the fleshly temptations that will come to you.

_____

_____

_____

PROJECT

In this journal keep a record of your fleshly activities for a least one week. A good Christian friend can help, but be ready to hear things you may not want to hear. Each day confess these sins and ask God to give you victory over the flesh.

_____

_____

_____

_____

_____

_____

_____

_____

_____

_____

_____

_____

_____

_____

_____

_____

_____

"Trust was foundational for our salvation, and it is equally foundational for our spiritual growth."

How do we know God will give us more grace gifts? In chapter one we looked at various passages of Scripture assuring us God wants to give us many more gifts. Yet, how can we be sure God can and will keep his promises?

To put it simply, can we trust God? Is it even necessary to trust God? In this chapter we are going to find out why the answer is an emphatic "YES!" Trust was foundational for our salvation, and it is equally foundational for our spiritual growth.

Peter admonishes us to,

"Always be prepared to give an answer to everyone who asks you to give the reason for the hope that you have" (1 Peter 3:15 NIV).

Some people have taken this to mean that we should have an answer ready for any question that anyone might ask us about God or the Bible. First, that is impossible and second, that is not what the verse says.

God tells us to be prepared to give an answer for the hope that we have. That word "hope" does not mean a wish for something that is uncertain.

Rather, it means to have a confident expectation in what is unseen or yet future. So, if people are asking us for a reason for our hope, they are wanting to know why we have confidence in God and his Word.

Personal

(Your thoughts, impressions and experiences)

"Believing in the goodness of God brings us courage."

In the context of this book we might ask, "Why are we confident God is going to continue his work within us?" The answer from chapter one would be, "Because God tells us in his Word, 'he will.'" But how do we know God can?

There are four attributes of God that are the basis for our hope: his goodness, his wisdom, his power and his faithfulness. We must believe that God has all four of these virtues or we will not trust God to continue his work within us.

God is Good
The first of these attributes is God's goodness. God's Word tells us he is good. King David, speaking of God, said,

"You are good and what you do is good" (Psalm 119:68 NIV). Four times in one Psalm David implores us to *"praise the Lord for His goodness"* (Psalm 107:8,15,21,31).

Believing in the goodness of God brings us courage. Again David wrote,

"I would have lost heart, unless I had believed that I would see the goodness of the Lord in the land of the living" (Psalm 27:13).

Because God is good he wants to give us good things. Our spiritual growth falls into that category. As I focus on the goodness of God, I can be confident God is going to do only good things for me.

(Your thoughts, impressions and experiences)

58

*"God's goodness would be meaningless
to us if he did not have the wisdom to give us what we need."*

God is All Wise

The second attribute that builds our confidence in God is his wisdom. God's goodness would be meaningless to us if he did not have the wisdom to give us what we need. His gifts would be random acts of goodness, but with no purpose behind them.

Again the Bible repeatedly reveals the wisdom of God.

Job stated,
> *"His wisdom is profound"*
> (Job 9:4 NIV)

and,
> *"To God
> belong wisdom and power;
> counsel and understanding
> are His"*
> (Job 12:13 NIV).

King David added,
> *"To Him,
> who by wisdom
> made the
> heavens"*
> (Psalm 136:5 NKJV).

This wisdom of God extends to us. The prophet Jeremiah, speaking to God's chosen people Israel, revealed,

> *"For I know
> the plans I have for
> you," declares the Lord, "plans
> to prosper you and not to harm you,
> plans to give you hope
> and a future"*
> (Jeremiah 29:11 NIV).

(Your thoughts, impressions and experiences)

"God is too wise to make mistakes."

God, in his great wisdom has a plan for us, too.

*"Do not conform
any longer to the pattern
of this world, but be transformed by the
renewing of your mind."*
(Romans 12:2 NIV).

*When you will be able to test
and approve what God's will is—
His good, pleasing and perfect will"*
(Romans 12:2 NIV).

Because we believe God is all knowing and all wise, we can be confident God knows exactly what we need, exactly when we need it. God is too wise to make mistakes.

God Is All-Powerful

The third attribute of God needed for us to rely upon him completely is his power. A God who is good and wise but without power would be too weak to carry out his good and wise plans.

Then it comes to describing the power of God, the Scriptures are filled with narrative. We see the power of God in the creation and sustaining of the universe.

"He made the earth by His power"
(Jeremiah 51:15 NIV).

Today he is

*"sustaining all things by
His powerful word"*
(Hebrews 1:3 NIV).

(Your thoughts, impressions and experiences)

CHAPTER FOUR
TRUSTING GOD FOR GODLINESS

"If we can trust God's power for our eternal salvation, can't we also trust him for the power to live the victorious Christian life?"

This power will never decline,

"He rules by His power forever"
(Psalm 66:7 NKJV).

We can trust the power of God to provide all that we need to grow in godliness. After all, we trusted God for the power to save us,

*"For
I am not ashamed
of the gospel of Christ,
for it is the power of God unto
salvation to every one that
believeth . . ."*
(Romans 1:16).

If we can trust God's power for our eternal salvation, can't we also trust him for the power to live the victorious Christian life?

God Is Faithful
The fourth attribute needed for us to have confidence in God is his faithfulness. If God were good, wise and powerful, but not faithful to do what he said he would do, then we would never know when to trust him.

Again there is no lack of Scripture to support the idea that God is faithful.

*"God,
who has called
you into fellowship with His Son
Jesus Christ,
is faithful"*
(1 Corinthians 1:9 NIV).

(Your thoughts, impressions and experiences)

"There is nothing outside God's control, so nothing catches him by surprise and affects his ability to keep his word."

"Because of the Lord's great love we are not consumed, for His compassions never fail. They are new every morning; great is your faithfulness" (Lamentations 3:22,23 NIV).

Because we are not in control of our circumstances, we are not always faithful to keep our promises. A father may promise his son to take him fishing on a certain day. When that day arrives the father may be lying on a hospital bed, unable to go fishing. We are not in control of our circumstances.

Why is God faithful? He is faithful because circumstances never change God. He is in control of all circumstances. There is nothing outside God's control, so nothing catches him by surprise and affects his ability to keep his word.

Why is God faithful? He is faithful also because he never changes. God's essence and his character remain the same.

"For I am the Lord, I do not change" (Malachi 3:6 NKJ).

"Every good gift and every perfect gift is from above, coming down from the Father of lights, with whom can be no variation, neither shadow that is cast by turning" (James 1:17 ASV).

(Your thoughts, impressions and experiences)

CHAPTER FOUR
TRUSTING GOD FOR GODLINESS

"Godliness is the foundational spiritual quality that makes the entire Christian life dynamic, effective and pleasing to God.

Because God is good, we can count on getting only good gifts from him. Because God is wise, we can count on getting the right gifts at the right time. Because God is powerful, we can count on his ability to come through for us. Because God is faithful, we can count on him to keep his promises to us.

Trusting God to Make Us Godly

Throughout this book we will be talking about godliness. Let's make sure we agree as to its meaning. We can define godliness as "God-like-ness." Scripture referred to godliness in such terms as

"filled with all the fulness of God"
(Ephesians 3:19),

"Christ formed in you"
(Galatians 4:19),

and
*"the stature
of the fulness
of Christ"*
(Ephesians 4:13).

Vine's Expository Dictionary of New Testament Words defines godliness this way, "Godliness denotes that piety which, characterized by a Godward attitude, does that which is well-pleasing to him."

Godliness is more than just a character trait. Godliness is the foundational spiritual quality that makes the entire Christian life dynamic, effective and pleasing to God. Godliness encompasses the entire Christian life and is the foundation for the building of all Christian character.

(Your thoughts, impressions and experiences)

63

"We can be humble without being godly, but we cannot be godly without being humble."

Once I felt I needed to be more loving, more kind and more at peace with my circumstances. These virtues are all good Christian character traits.

Unfortunately, the result was that when I focused on one virtue, I slipped behind in the others. Again, I was getting the cart before the horse. Godliness comes before virtue.

When we put our sole focus on being more godly, we find that the virtues automatically follow. We can be humble without being godly, but we cannot be godly without being humble.

No greater compliment can be paid to a Christian than to call him or her a godly person. It is better than being called a dynamic speaker or talented singer. It is better than being a loving father or a law-abiding citizen. At my funeral I hope people will be able to say honestly, "Cal was a godly man."

The Value of Godliness

In 1 Timothy the apostle Paul makes two comments to Timothy about the value of godliness. The first benefit is found in chapter four, verse eight,

"For physical training is of some value, but godliness has value for all things, holding promise for both the present life and the life to come"
(1 Timothy 4:8 NIV).

Notice the two times godliness is profitable, in the present life and in the future life. In the present life godliness is the gateway to God's blessings.

(Your thoughts, impressions and experiences)

"The godly believer lays up treasures in heaven."

There is no other way for believers to receive God's grace gifts than through growing in godliness. As our relationship with God deepens, we find the desire and the power to change our outward behavior that has enslaved us.

Godliness is also the key to an intimate relationship with God. As we become more like him, we find we want to spend more time with him.

We share common values, concerns and interests with God. We always like to be with people who are like us, and we will enjoy being with God more when we are more Godlike (godly).

The second value of godliness, found in 1 Timothy 4:8, is in the life to come. When this life is over we will all stand before God and be judged,

*"For we must
all appear before the judgment seat
of Christ . . ."*
(2 Corinthians 5:10).

Here God will reward us for the good we have done while on earth (1 Corinthians 3:13-15). Those aspects of our lives judged as worthless are destroyed and only the good remains.

The godly believer lays up treasures in heaven (Matthew 6:20). In contrast, the Christian whose focus has been on the physical and material will lose the rewards for his or her earthly efforts. The Bible indicates that these rewards will be important to us. So those who grow in godliness will profit in heaven too.

(Your thoughts, impressions and experiences)

*"First is the devotion and then,
and only then, is the correct behavior possible."*

The apostle Paul also told Timothy,

*"But godliness
with contentment is
great gain"*
(1 Timothy 6:6).

The gain is not just a little gain, or some gain, it is great gain. This word "great" means exceedingly great or mighty. Hebrews 8:11 translates the same word "the greatest." There is no greater gain in this life than personal godliness.

Examples of Godliness
In the book of Genesis we have a great example of a godly man. His name was Enoch. The record reads

"Enoch walked with God"
(Genesis 5:22,24).

Enoch enjoyed a close personal relationship with God. It was the type of relationship that Adam and Eve had with God before they sinned (Genesis 3:8). Enoch was devoted to God.

In a chapter in the New Testament, often called "Faith's Hall of Fame," God praises Enoch for his faith.

*"By faith Enoch was taken
from this life, so that he did not
experience death; he could not be
found, because
God had taken him away.
For before he was taken, he was
commended as one
who pleased God"*
(Hebrews 11:5 NIV).

(Your thoughts, impressions and experiences)

CHAPTER FOUR
TRUSTING GOD FOR GODLINESS

"Sometimes we judge God's ability on the basis of our inability."

Enoch never tasted the bitterness of death because he pleased God. Enoch's attitude of being devoted to God resulted in his actions of pleasing God. First is the devotion and then, and only then, is the correct behavior possible.

DECISION TIME

We trusted God to give us eternal life, but can we trust him to give us his abundant life? Sometimes we judge God's ability on the basis of our inability. Because we fail, we doubt God's ability to give us the power to succeed. The goal of this chapter is to help us see that we can trust God to produce his godliness within us. Now, are you willing to do it?

Be honest with God about how you feel right now. If you are feeling defeated in your attempts to live a godly life, tell God. But, then tell God that you believe he can do what you can't do, empower you to live a godly life. Ask God to increase your trust in him. Ask God to show you his power in your life.

(Your thoughts, impressions and experiences)

CHAPTER FOUR
QUESTIONS AND DISCUSSION

1. List the four attributes of God that are the basis for our confidence in him.
   a.
   b.
   c.
   d.

2. Which of these four attributes is the most significant to you in learning to trust God more? Why?

   _____

   _____

   _____

   _____

3. In your own words, define godliness.

   _____

   _____

   _____

   _____

4. How important is being godly to you?

   _____

   _____

   _____

5. What truth did you learn about godliness from Enoch?

   _____

   _____

PROJECT

Every relationship is built upon trust. Where would you place yourself on a scale of 1 to 10, with 1 being just trusting God for eternal life and 10 being trusting God for everything in your life?

_____

_____

_____

_____

_____

_____

_____

_____

For one week keep track of the times you trusted or failed to trust God for something. Disobedience to God is the primary evidence of lack of trust in God. Confess these sins as a lack of trust and review the major points of this chapter to remind yourself why you can trust God.

_____

_____

_____

_____

_____

_____

_____

_____

ADDITIONAL JOURNALING

"God will resist everything pride does to produce spirituality."

Without humility there can be no spiritual growth. Pride, the opposite of humility, keeps us from all of God's blessings. Twice Scripture tells us,

> *"God opposes the proud, but gives grace to the humble"*
> (1 Peter 5:5; James 4:6 NIV).

God is never against the believer. God is for us. God opposes the pride within us.

God will resist everything pride does to produce spirituality. The reason is that the proud person is trying to grow in the energy of the flesh. We saw in chapter two that the flesh is the enemy of God. God is not going to give his support and aid to something that opposes his will.

I have met Christians who were relying on themselves to become more spiritual. They had their list of do's and don'ts. They had their regimen of "spiritual disciplines" they were counting on to make themselves spiritual. Sadly, for all their trying, they were also failing.

We have seen all of God's blessings come to us by his grace. Since God "gives grace to the humble," humility is important for receiving all of God's blessings.

Humility was a necessary attitude for our salvation. We had to humbly acknowledge we were sinners and could not save ourselves. We then had to put our complete trust in Jesus to save us. All of these actions revealed an inward humility.

(Your thoughts, impressions and experiences)

*"The same pride which keeps
people from receiving God's gift of eternal life
also keeps believers from receiving the rest of God's grace gifts"*

Pride keeps people out of heaven. Some people believe they are good enough to get to heaven <u>by</u> their good works. That is an evidence of pride. Some people know they are not good enough <u>now</u> to go to heaven but are planning to change some habits to make themselves better. That, <u>too</u>, is pride. One man I talked to about the Lord, and his need of salvation, said he wanted to go to hell. He would not receive "charity" from anyone, and that included God. This is an example of extreme pride.

The same pride which keeps people from receiving God's gift of eternal life also keeps believers from receiving the rest of God's grace gifts. We want to impress God and other Christians with <u>our</u> ability to live the Christian life. So we go out and try to make it happen ourselves.

The problem with our trying to live the Christian life is that we can't. In trying, we are doomed to failure. The reason for our failure is that our trying is an evidence of pride and "God resists the proud." As much as God wants us to have victory over sin, God will oppose victory if we try to accomplish it in our own strength. The Bible says Christ is our victory,

*"But thanks be to God, which
giveth us the victory through our
Lord Jesus Christ"*
(1 Corinthians 15:57 KJV).

God will allow the world, the flesh and the devil to block our peace, joy and rest to teach us his lessons and to conform us to Christ.

(Your thoughts, impressions and experiences)

"We did not ask God to help us save ourselves, nor can we ask God to help us give ourselves victory over sin."

I have heard defeated Christians say, "Why won't God help me? I am trying to get victory over my sin addiction. I am asking God to help me, but he doesn't. How come?" There may be several biblical principles at play in their lives, but often the answer is found in their own words, "I am trying . . . ."

When we say, "I am trying ..." to God and then ask for his help, what we are really saying is, "God, I'll do most of the work, You just help me where I am weak." Is that how we got saved?

Did we say to God, "God, I'll do 90% of the work of saving myself, and You fill in the other 10%." No! We said, "God, I can't do anything to save myself, so I am trusting You completely for my salvation." We did not ask God to help us save ourselves, nor can we ask God to help us give ourselves victory over sin.

Prayers to God for victory over sin need to begin something like, "God, I can't do this. Apart from your power I am totally and completely helpless here. I am through trying and now I am trusting you for the victory."

How God Produces Humility Within Us

God, being the loving, caring and wise God he is, knows we all need help in becoming more humble. Therefore, God has devised some very creative ways to produce humility within us. These are also grace gifts, although we seldom think of them that way. Here are a few humility-producing "gifts."

(Your thoughts, impressions and experiences)

73

*"Nothing humbles us more
quickly than being overwhelmed with problems."*

1. A major problem or lots of little ones

Nothing humbles us more quickly than being overwhelmed with problems. It might be a major problem, something that threatens life and limb, or it might be a ton of little problems. Minor financial problems, combined with minor home problems, compounded by minor health problems can add up to as much anxiety as one major problem.

Elijah knew what it was like to be overwhelmed with problems and God used it to produce humility in him. In 1 Kings 19 we read how God dealt with Elijah. Elijah had just experienced a great victory over the prophets of Baal. Elijah had prayed for God to prove his great power and God answered Elijah's prayer mightily.

Fire from heaven consumed Elijah's water-soaked offering, the wood, the stones, the dust and the water. Then the people killed every prophet of Baal. It was a great victory.

Beware of victories; they can lead to pride. A few years back I spoke at a national convention for a particular group of Christians.

After I finished speaking, a pastor who is a fine speaker himself came up to me enthusiastically and exclaimed, "That was the finest sermon I have ever heard at our national convention, and I've been to most of them."

(Your thoughts, impressions and experiences)

"By focusing on his circumstances, [Elijah] lost sight of God's power."

It just so happened I had prayed more about that sermon than I had ever prayed over any one sermon in my life.

God had honored my prayers and gave me just the right words and the ability to speak them with power. So, I was also very pleased with the content and the delivery. Right away pride set in. Satan took a victory given by God and used it to tempt me with pride. Unfortunately, I bought it—hook, line and sinker.

If it is any consolation, I am not the only person to fall for that trick; Elijah did, too. After the defeat of the prophets of Baal, the wicked queen Jezebel swore to kill Elijah. Elijah ran (literally) into the desert to hide from Jezebel. Here, in the desert, we see two evidences of pride in Elijah.

Sitting under a juniper tree Elijah prayed,

"Now, O Lord, take away my life" (1 Kings 19:4).

Elijah wanted to die. Why? Some have suggested that Elijah felt he had done his greatest deed for God and now wanted God to reward him by going to heaven. That would be an evidence of pride.

However, we need to take note of Elijah's attitude here. Elijah was not gloating over his victory, rather, he was depressed over his circumstances.

(Your thoughts, impressions and experiences)

"Trials and tribulation can reveal our pride and humble us quickly."

Elijah had a problem too big to handle. By focusing on his circumstances, he lost sight of God's power. Rather than seeking the power of God, Elijah was content to wallow in his own weakness. That is a form of pride.

Another evidence of pride comes quickly after his prayer. In a conversation with God Elijah says,

"I have been very zealous for the Lord God Almighty ... and I am the only one left ..."
(1 Kings 19:10 NIV).

How it must sadden the heart of God to hear his children claim to be the only ones who are right. "Our denomination has the corner on truth." Or, "Only we, who don't belong to any denomination, are right." Such statements come from a heart of pride and arrogance.

Elijah had a pride problem, but God had a grace gift. The gift was Jezebel's threat on his life. That threat is what drove Elijah out into the desert where God could meet and talk with him. God showed Elijah he wasn't God's only follower. There were seven thousand others who worshiped God. God told Elijah that he would not die, but instead, death would come to Jezebel and her husband, Ahab.

God dealt with Elijah's pride and he used a major problem to do it. By his grace God can and will deal with our pride, too.

(Your thoughts, impressions and experiences)

"God will use, and even cause, physical suffering to deal with our pride."

Perhaps he will use an outside threat, as with Elijah, (a problem too big for us to handle, bringing us to our knees). Trials and tribulation can reveal our pride and humble us quickly.

2. Sickness or a physical problem
Sometimes God uses minor <u>physical</u> problems to deal with our pride. In the past six years I have had eight kidney stones.

They say a kidney stone attack compares to labor pain. I have never had labor pains, but my wife has on three separate occasions. I remember when she was getting ready to deliver one of our children, I was thinking, "Boy, I'm sure glad God made me a man." You see, I hate pain. I do everything possible to avoid pain.

But God, in his infinite wisdom, decided that I needed some pain in my life, so he made my body produce kidney stones. Some people have a hard time believing God produces pain. King David didn't;

*"I know,
O LORD, that your
laws are righteous, and in
faithfulness <u>you
have afflicted
me</u>"*
(Psalm 119:75 NIV).

Pain is not always bad. Because of the pain of a woman's labor, a child is born. Because of the pain inflicted in surgery, a cancer is cut out. Pain with a purpose is good.

(Your thoughts, impressions and experiences)

*"God will use, and even cause,
physical suffering to deal with our pride."*

God will use, and even cause, physical suffering to deal with our pride.

The apostle Paul is a good example of being given physical suffering to defeat pride. Because of the abundance of special revelations given to him, Paul could have become extremely proud. But God, in his grace, dealt with Paul's potential for pride through physical suffering.

"I will say this: because these experiences I had were so tremendous, God was afraid I might <u>be puffed up</u> by them; so I was given a physical condition which has been a thorn in my flesh, a messenger from Satan to hurt and bother me and prick my pride"
(2 Corinthians 12:7 TLB).

In the Greek, the language in which the New Testament was originally written, the word for "given" is also the word for grace. God, in his grace, gave Paul physical suffering. Satan wanted to use the condition to hurt and bother Paul, but God wanted to use it to deal with Paul's pride.

Paul's initial response was to ask God to remove this affliction from him,

"Three different times I asked God to make me well again"
(2 Corinthians 12:8 TLB).

But God did not heal Paul. It is not God's will that everybody be healed. In all likelihood Paul suffered from this affliction until the day he died.

(Your thoughts, impressions and experiences)

78

"Physical weakness can destroy personal pride."

God gave the affliction to Paul to deal with his pride, or the potential for pride.

So how did Paul feel about this physical suffering? Paul sums it up this way,

*"Now I am glad
to boast about how
weak I am; I am glad to be a
living demonstration of Christ's power,
instead of showing off my own power
and abilities"*
(2 Corinthians 12:9 TLB).

Physical weakness can destroy personal pride. I have had kidney stone attacks while eating in a restaurant. I have had kidney stone attacks while preaching.

There is not a trip I take, either on vacation or when doing the Lord's business, where I am not aware that at a moment's notice my body might be filled with pain.

Every time I step aboard an airplane, I wonder if we will have to make an emergency landing somewhere to cart me off to a hospital.

In the illustration of "my great sermon" earlier, all God had to do was remind me of how weak I am.

One way God does that is through physical suffering. It is pain, but it is pain with a purpose.

(Your thoughts, impressions and experiences)

*"Pride causes us to tell
God what he can or cannot do."*

_____

_____

_____

_____

_____

_____

_____

_____

_____

_____

_____

_____

_____

_____

_____

_____

(Your thoughts, impressions and experiences)

3. **A failure**

Failure is one experience we all have in common. If we think of failure as anything that is not perfect, then we fail much more than we succeed. But there is a difference between common failure and "gut-wrenching" failure. The latter type is the kind God uses to defeat pride in our lives.

The apostle Peter had a pride problem. Peter thought he was a little bit better than all the other disciples. Peter was the first disciple to acknowledge that Christ was the Son of God (Matthew 16:16). After this acknowledgment, Christ promised Peter the keys to the kingdom. Shortly afterward Peter showed evidence of pride.

Jesus began teaching his disciples he had to die and be raised from the dead (Matthew 16:21). But Peter would have none of it;

> *"Peter
> took him aside
> and began to rebuke him,
> 'Never, Lord!' he said.
> 'This shall never
> happen to
> you'"*
> (Matthew 16:22 NIV).

What Peter thought was an expression of love was really an expression of pride. Pride causes us to tell God what he can or cannot do.

Jesus pointed out Peter's pride clearly.

80

CHAPTER FIVE
HUMILITY

"Jesus used Peter's failure to address his pride."

"Jesus turned and said to Peter, 'Get behind me Satan. You are a stumbling block to me; you do not have in mind the things of God, but the things of men'"
(Matthew 16:23 NIV).

Then turning to all the disciples Jesus said,

"If anyone would come after me, he must deny himself and take up his cross and follow me"
(Matthew 16:24).

"Denying self" and "taking up your cross" are terms that speak of the death of self and pride. Jesus used Peter's failure to address his pride.

There was another time in Peter's life where God used a personal failure to humble him. Just before his arrest and crucifixion, Jesus ate a last supper with the disciples. Jesus told his disciples they would all desert him soon.

"'You will all fall away' Jesus told them"
(Mark 14:27 NIV).

There was one disciple who, lifted up with pride, said,

"Even if all fall away, I will not"
(Mark 14:29).

Peter again thought he was better than the other disciples. Jesus told Peter he would fall away with the rest, but Peter refused to believe him.

_____
_____
_____
_____
_____
_____
_____
_____
_____
_____
_____
_____
_____
_____
_____
_____
_____

(Your thoughts, impressions and experiences)

81

*"[Peter] was reduced to tears
and his pride was reduced to ashes."*

_____

_____

_____

_____

_____

_____

_____

_____

_____

_____

_____

_____

_____

_____

_____

(Your thoughts, impressions and experiences)

Even the other disciples joined in with Peter. So Jesus told Peter when, how, and how often he would fall (Mark 14:30). Sure enough, Peter denied the Lord three times before the night was over. Peter's denial was one of the greatest personal failures in the Bible. In the end, Peter was humbled. He was reduced to tears and his pride was reduced to ashes.

Failure is never pleasant. My first two ministries were failures in anybody's book. I had all the theological training and degree, but I didn't see my pride. To make me usable, God had to deal with the pride. Those ministry failures were the means God used to begin his work in me, conforming me into the image of Christ and bringing me to a level of spiritual maturity where my actions, directed by the Holy Spirit, are pleasing to him.

4. Sin

I believe the Bible. I take it literally unless it says otherwise. One of the passages we must take literally is Romans 8:28,

*"And we know
<u>all things</u>
work
together for good ..."*
(Romans 8:28).

Now I believe "all things" means <u>ALL</u> things, which includes sin. But how can sin be good?

Sin is not good, but God can use sin to accomplish his good purposes.

CHAPTER FIVE
HUMILITY

"The crucifixion of Jesus was the greatest injustice ever committed on the face of the earth, but God used it to provide our salvation."

The crucifixion of Jesus was the greatest injustice ever committed on the face of the earth, but God used it to provide our salvation. In like manner, God can use our sins to destroy our pride.

When we think of great sinners in the Bible, we have to think of King David, whose greatest sin is detailed in 2 Samuel 11. Not only did David commit adultery with Bathsheba, but he also covered it up by murdering her husband (vv. 4, 15-17). Why did David think he could get away with these crimes? Did King David think he was better than everyone else? In fact, he did! David was the king. He was subject to no human control. He could have <u>anything</u> he wanted and <u>anybody</u> he wanted, <u>too</u>. His pride fed off his power. Because of his great power, David's egotism was out of control.

But there was one thing David forgot. Although he was not subject to any human control, David was still answerable to God. God sent his prophet Nathan to confront David. Nathan walked into David's court and pronounced David guilty of sinning against God:

"Why have you despised the commandment of the Lord, to do evil in His sight?
You have killed Uriah, the Hittite, with the sword, you have taken his wife to be your wife..."
(2 Samuel 12:9).

(Your thoughts, impressions and experiences)

"With pride defeated we become better servants of God."

_____

_____

_____

_____

_____

_____

_____

_____

_____

_____

_____

_____

_____

_____

(Your thoughts, impressions and experiences)

Nathan then pronounced God's judgment upon David. David then realized something which his pride had blinded him to before. The king was accountable to God for his actions. Although the king could never be tried in a human court, the man David could not escape God's judgment.

In the end we find God used this sin and resulting judgment for good in David's life. David repented,

"I have sinned against the Lord"
(2 Samuel 12:13).

After he repented he was brought back to a position of humility and trust in God.

At the end of his life, David humbly said this about God,

"Yours, O Lord is the greatness and the power and the glory and the majesty and the splendor, for everything in heaven and earth is yours. Yours, O Lord, is the kingdom; you are exalted as head over all"
(1 Chronicles 29:11 NIV).

We are often quick to judge those who fall into sin. We want to write sinners off as God's rejects. Sinners may never escape the consequences of their sin, as David never completely escaped his, but God can use sin to defeat pride. With pride defeated we become better servants of God.

"The first evidence of true humility can be seen in a recognition of the ruling authority of God through his Word."

I am sure there are more ways God can conquer pride and produce humility within us. These are just four he has used on me most. I have been very guilty of pride and needful of every way God, in his love, has sought to break it.

Evidences of Humility

How can we tell if we are humble? I once prayed, "Lord, <u>keep</u> me humble." My wife, hearing my prayer, responded, "Lord, <u>make</u> him humble first!" She must have been kidding. I have, personally, been very proud of my humility!!!???

All kidding aside, there are certain evidences of humility that we can see without becoming proud. They fall into two categories: evidences of humility in our relationship with God, and evidences of humility in our relationships with others.

Toward God

1. Submission to the authority of God

The first evidence of true humility can be seen in a recognition of the ruling authority of God through his Word. Pride makes self the ruling authority in all matters of life. Whenever we need to make a decision, we just ask ourselves, "What do I want?" There is no higher authority than our self-centered desires.

Humility, on the other hand, submits to God's authority. It is no longer, "What do I want?" but, "what does God want here?" We limit our freedom, making it submissive to God's will.

(Your thoughts, impressions and experiences)

"We find God's will in God's Word."

We find God's will in God's Word.

With Biblical humility in place, we go to God's Word with the attitude of, "Whatever God says, I will do." When God's Word conflicts with our will, we yield to God's Word.

Refusing to acknowledge the authority of the Word of God is an evidence of a lack of humility. When we know the Bible tells us not to lie (Colossians 3:9), but we choose to lie anyway, we are not submitting to the ruling authority of the Word of God. The same is true for adultery, hatred, murder, drunkenness, disorderliness, etc. I am not talking about those times when sin sneaks up behind us and grabs us unawares. I'm talking about those times when we deliberately choose to live contrary to the Word of God.

This may explain why,

"God resists the proud but gives grace to the humble"
(James 4:6; 1 Peter 5:5).

How can God give his grace gifts to those who refuse to submit to the ruling authority of his Word? Without submission we are not in the place where we can use his gifts, for we are still <u>living for self</u>. God's grace gifts are given to bring greater glory to God, not to self.

2. **Submission to living by faith**
No less than four times the Bible tells us,

(Your thoughts, impressions and experiences)

86

"Humility chooses to believe God."

"The just shall live by faith"
(Habakkuk 2:4; Romans 1:17;
Galatians 3:11; Hebrews 10:38).

If we need any more convincing, God obliges us saying,

"For we walk by faith, not by sight"
(2 Corinthians 5:7).

There is a whole chapter coming in this book on the topic of faith. For now, we need to see that humility chooses to believe God. Pride looks at the circumstances, the things we see, and makes decisions accordingly. Pride says, "If I can't understand it, I won't believe it."

Faith chooses to believe God and acts accordingly, even if believing defies logic.

Many believers recognize the authority of the Word of God but do not respond in faith to its teachings. When we read,

"Do not be anxious about anything"
(Philippians 4:6 NKJV),

in humility believers respond by not worrying.

Or, if we read,

"In everything give thanks ..."
(1 Thessalonians 5:18),

the genuinely humble believer immediately gives thanks, even for the testings, trials and tribulations of life.

(Your thoughts, impressions and experiences)

*"Paul said everything he was,
or ever hoped to be, he owed to the grace of God."*

3. **Submission to the grace of God**
The apostle Paul was arguably the greatest of the apostles. Paul's writings compose most of our New Testament. He probably led more people to Christ than any other person of his time. Yet, this great man said this about himself,

*"But by the grace of God
I am what I am: and His grace
which was bestowed upon me was
not found vain; but I labored more
abundantly than they all; yet not I,
but the grace of God which
was with me"*
(1 Corinthians 15:10 ASV).

To what did Paul owe his success? Was it his family training? Education? Self-discipline? Religious upbringing? No! Paul said everything he was, or ever hoped to be, he owed to the grace of God.

Pride causes us to want to take credit for what God has done for us. There are no self-made women or men. Why am I able to write this book? First, I was born in a country where I have the freedom to write. What did I do to deserve that? Nothing; therefore it is a gift of God's grace. Second, I have the mental capacity to think, analyze and synthesize information. This mental ability is something God gave me, again a gift of his grace. Third, I have the Holy Spirit living within me to teach, guide and direct me as I write, another gift of God's grace.

(Your thoughts, impressions and experiences)

"There are many more
elements that have all come together to
make this book possible, all by the grace of God."

There are many more elements that have all come together to make this book possible, all by the grace of God.

Humble believers acknowledge that God's grace is the sole reason for all their successes. There is no room for boasting and bragging about self. Were it not for the grace of God, we would still be the enemies of God (Ephesians 2:11-13).

Submission to the grace of God has another dimension as well. When Paul prayed for God to remove his "thorn in the flesh," God's answer was,

"My grace
is sufficient
for you"
(2 Corinthians 12:9 NIV).

In other words, God is saying, "I will not remove the thorn, but I will give you my grace that will enable you to live with it." Then God told Paul which particular grace gift he would get,

"My power
is made perfect in
weakness"
(2 Corinthians 12:9 NIV).

God's grace gift would be his supernatural power at work in Paul's weakness. In humility Paul submitted himself to this grace. How do we know he did? Listen to Paul's answer to God,

(Your thoughts, impressions and experiences)

89

"Pride does not submit to the grace of God."

_____

_____

_____

_____

_____

_____

_____

_____

_____

_____

_____

_____

_____

_____

_____

_____

_____

(Your thoughts, impressions and experiences)

90

"Therefore I will boast all the more gladly about my weakness, so that Christ's power might rest upon me. That is why, for Christ's sake, I delight in weakness, in insults, in hardships, in persecutions, in difficulties. For when I am weak, then am I strong"
(2 Corinthians 12:9-10 NIV).

Pride does not submit to the grace of God. When testings, trials and tribulations come, pride fights and kicks, refusing to allow God's grace to "be sufficient." The writer of Hebrews warns us,

"See to it that no one misses the grace of God and that no bitter root grows up to cause trouble and defile many"
(Hebrews 12:15 NIV).

I have met Christians who have refused to receive God's grace. Perhaps an insensitive fellow-believer hurt them. At the time of need God offered his grace, but rather than submit to the provision of God's grace, the hurt individual allowed pride to be in control. The person became angry and bitter and passed that anger and bitterness on to others. In refusing the grace of God, we end up negatively influencing other believers.

4. **Submission to the timing of God**
Allowing God to do his work in his time is another evidence of humility. One thing I have learned in over 30 years of ministry is that God never operates on my timetable!

"Humility is willingness to believe that God knows the right time."

Sometimes I get so impatient with God; it seems he is soooo slow. Other times God is going much faster than I want. God's timing is always right. That is because he always knows when the time's right. For over a thousand years Israelites prayed for the Messiah. At just the right time God sent him,

*"But when
the right time
came, the time God
decided upon, he sent
His son ..."*
(Galatians 4:4 TLB).

Christ's death was also at the right time,

*"You see,
at just the right time,
when we were still powerless,
Christ died for
the ungodly"*
(Romans 5:6 NIV).

Just as God knew the right time to send his Son, so God knows just the right time to send his other grace gifts to us. Humility is willingness to believe that God knows the right time.

*"Humble yourselves,
therefore, under the mighty hand of
God, that he may exalt you
in due time"*
(1 Peter 5:6).

"Due time" is the right time. Humility submits to waiting for the right time.

(Your thoughts, impressions and experiences)

"Sometimes it hurts to wait."

Several years ago I had the opportunity to talk with Sam Vinton, Sr., who has served the Lord faithfully as a missionary to Zaire/Congo for over seventy years. He went to the Belgian Congo in 1929 and stayed throughout revolution, rebellion and civil wars.

Often the forces of darkness surrounded him, but his light never flickered for a moment. He buried his wife and a daughter in Africa. I asked him what was the hardest thing God ever asked him to do.

I thought it might have something to do with living on very little income, or seeing his young daughter die miles from needed medical help. But his answer was a total surprise to me. *"The hardest thing God has ever asked me to do,"* he replied, *"was to wait."* He then told about first going to the mission field, young and full of energy to do great things for God. God prevented him from getting started for months. *"The wait was agonizing. We wanted to get going and do something, but all we could do was wait for God to open the doors for us to get started."*

Often it is hard to wait. Sometimes it hurts to wait. We want to see a loved one saved or we want victory over sin, right now! We want all of God's power right away, so we can do great things for him. We don't understand why we have to wait. In our pride we want to take over and make things happen ourselves. Humility submits to the timetable of God.

(Your thoughts, impressions and experiences)

92

"When our suffering is for Christ, we can even glory in it."

5. **Submission to undeserved suffering**

There are two types of suffering in life. There is deserved suffering and undeserved suffering.

Deserved suffering is the suffering we bring upon ourselves because of something we have done. A thief may be imprisoned because of his crime. A murderer may be put to death. A liar may be exposed and shunned. This is deserved suffering.

But, there is another type of suffering. Suffering we may have to endure, but not for anything we have done. This type of suffering would qualify as "pain with a purpose."

When our suffering is for Christ, we can even glory in it.

"But let none of you suffer as a murderer, a thief, an evildoer, or as a busybody in other people's matters. Yet if anyone suffers as a Christian, let him not be ashamed, but let him glorify God in this matter"
(1 Peter 4:15-16 NKJV).

In his second epistle to the Corinthians, the apostle Paul shared two benefits of suffering. First he said,

"(God) comforts us in all our troubles, so that we can comfort those in any trouble with the comfort we ourselves have received from God"
(2 Corinthians 1:4 NIV).

_____
_____
_____
_____
_____
_____
_____
_____
_____
_____
_____
_____
_____
_____
_____
_____
_____
_____

(Your thoughts, impressions and experiences)

93

*"Undeserved suffering helps
us trust self less and God more."*

_____

_____

_____

_____

_____

_____

_____

_____

_____

_____

_____

_____

_____

_____

(Your thoughts, impressions and experiences)

God comforts us as we go through the trials and tribulations of life. Then as we witness others struggling through their trials, we can come alongside to share our comfort with them.

When Paul, speaking of a very severe trial, said,

*"Yes, we had the sentence
of death in ourselves, that we should
not trust in ourselves but in God who
raises the dead"*
(2 Corinthians 1:9 NKJV).

Undeserved suffering helps us trust self less and God more. The humble believer responds, "I am willing to suffer if God can use it to make me more godly or more usable to him." Pride refuses to submit to the grace of suffering.

How many times have we heard Christians say, "Never pray for patience!" Why? It is because they know the only way to grow in patience is to go through tribulation,

"tribulation worketh patience"
(Romans 5:3).

What are we really saying when we exclaim, "Never pray for patience!"?

We are saying, "The gain is not worth the pain!" Our pride keeps us from submitting to the hand of God in allowing suffering into our lives.

CHAPTER FIVE
HUMILITY

"In our pride we want to win arguments, promote self and do for others in order <u>to get</u> for self."

Toward Others

The second major evidence of true humility can be seen in our submission to others. As we grow in humility we will want to serve and minister to people. Prideful, self-centered wants will be exchanged for a true care and concern for others. God's Word tells us,

"Submit to one another out of reverence for Christ"
(Ephesians 5:21 NIV).

Also,

"Do nothing out of selfish ambition or vain conceit, but in humility consider others better than yourselves"
(Philippians 2:3 NIV).

This goes against our prideful, natural tendencies.

In our pride we want to win arguments, promote self and do for others in order <u>to get</u> for self. We want to be on the top of the heap. Because we are self-centered, we do not want to serve others. Rather, we want to be served.

As a pastor, I see this lack of humility evidenced by some men in their relationship with their wives. The husband comes home from work and wants the "little woman" to wait on him "hand and foot."

(Your thoughts, impressions and experiences)

*"When humility is firmly in place,
we find we have an unconditional commitment
to serve others."*

His wife is the 21st century version of the 18th century American slave. He wants to be "king of his castle." The husband then justifies his proud attitude by quoting Scripture to his wife,

*"Wives, submit yourselves unto
your own husbands, as unto the Lord"*
(Ephesians 5:22).

The husband's obligation is found three verses later,

*"Husbands, love your wives, even
as Christ also loved the church and
gave himself for it"*
(Ephesians 5:25).

`How much did Christ love us, the church? Christ gave up all his rights and privileges to meet our needs. The death of the Son of God on the cross was the sacrifice of all sacrifices. How dare men treat their wives like slaves! That is not how Christ treats us!

When humility is firmly in place, we find we have an unconditional commitment to serve others. We are especially committed to the spiritual development of those around us. We want to see believers grow in their relationship with God. Ministry is not an obligation but a passion that involves us in the lives of other people.

The first step of any true ministry is a commitment to the success of others. Their growth, their success, and meeting their needs becomes our highest priority.

(Your thoughts, impressions and experiences)

CHAPTER FIVE
HUMILITY

"Humility is not something we ask for and the next morning we wake up with all evidence of pride gone."

Any ministry, motivated to meet our own needs, is going to fail. God does not bless pride. He resists it!

DECISION TIME

This chapter begins with, "Without humility there can be no spiritual growth." We must come to the place where we are absolutely convinced of the truth of this statement.

Our pride would keep us from believing this truth, but we must agree with God here or we will never grow in our walk with him.

Take a few moments to talk with God about the importance of humility and your desire to be humble.

Humility is not something we ask for and the next morning we wake up with all evidence of pride gone. There is a process of being made humble that involves pain with a purpose. Share honestly with God your willingness for him to use the following to produce humility within you:
1. A major problem or lots of little ones
2. Sickness or a physical problem
3. Failure
4. Sin

Ask God to show you evidence of pride in your relationship with him and your relationships with others. These can be part of the "failures" God will use to produce more humility.

(Your thoughts, impressions and experiences)

CHAPTER FIVE
QUESTIONS AND DISCUSSION

1. Why does God "resist the proud and give grace to the humble"?

   _Proud _____ _____ Things_

   Pride and build walls

2. What is wrong with saying, "I am trying to live for God"?

   _Trusting God _____ _____ _____ _____

   _4:6_

3. List four ways God can produce humility in us.
   a.
   b. _sin,_
   c.
   d.

4. Which one(s) has God been using on you?

   sin,

5. List the five evidences of humility toward God.
   a. _humility_
   b. _fear_
   c. _learning_
   d.
   e.

6. Based on these five evidences, how would you rate your humility toward God?

_____

_____

_____

_____

7. Is the end result of becoming more humble worth the process needed in its development?

_____

_____

_____

_____

PROJECT

In building our relationship with Christ, nothing puts the brakes on harder and faster than pride. But, pride is very hard to see in ourselves. Therefore, we need to ask God to reveal it to us. Set aside no less than one hour and ask God to reveal evidences of pride in you. Begin reading in the Word of God (I recommend Philippians or James). Read slowly, asking God to reveal areas of pride. Any area of disobedience has its roots in pride. Record these prideful attitudes or actions. Confess them to God and ask God for the humility to submit completely to his will.

ADDITIONAL JOURNALING

"Spiritual maturity is a product of grace."

SIX ELEMENTS
OF GODLY OBEDIENCE

1. **Know the Word of God**
2. **Understand the Word of God**
3. **Believe the Word of God**
4. **Desire to obey the Word of God**
5. **Empowered to obey the Word of God**
6. **Obedience to the Word of God**

In the first section of this book we studied some major doctrines concerning spiritual growth. We know God began a good work in us and know he will carry it on to completion (Philippians 1:6).

God saved us by his grace, so we cannot boast about what we did to earn everlasting life (Ephesians 2:8-9). The same is true for our Christian growth. Spiritual maturity is a product of grace, so we can't boast about what we did to achieve godliness, either. Our salvation is a work of God, and so also is our spiritual growth.

Although our spiritual maturity is a work of God's grace, we don't automatically grow spiritually. Achieving spiritual growth parallels the way we became saved. Although salvation is a free gift, we are not automatically saved. In both cases man has certain responsibilities. These responsibilities are not fleshly works but Spirit-led responses of faith.

Over the next six chapters we are going to look at the elements of Godly obedience listed above. We are going to see God has certain responsibilities and we have other responsibilities.

(Your thoughts, impressions and experiences)

"Spiritual growth begins with the knowledge of God's Word."

We need to be careful not to make two mistakes here. The first is not fulfilling our responsibilities. Knowing our responsibilities and doing them are two different things. Many people try to intellectualize biblical truths. Truths must be acted upon, not just known.

The second mistake we could make is in trying to assume for ourselves God's responsibilities. We can't do God's job. We haven't the power or the wisdom. We will fall flat on our faces if we try to do what only God can do.

The First Element: Know the Word of God

Spiritual growth begins with the knowledge of God's Word. Often the apostle Paul stated he was writing things to his readers so they would not be ignorant. Concerning the special stewardship for the church Paul wrote,

"I do not want you to be ignorant of this mystery, brothers"
(Romans 11:25 NIV).

Regarding the important issue of spiritual gifts Paul said,

"Now concerning spiritual gifts, brethren, I would not have you ignorant"
(1 Corinthians 12:1).

Referring to the death of a believer, Paul comforts us with

"But I would not have you to be ignorant, brethren, concerning them who are asleep"
(1 Thessalonians 4:13).

(Your thoughts, impressions and experiences)

"The Word of God reveals the will of God."

Without knowledge we have no starting point nor foundation upon which to build. Knowledge must come first. The first step in our salvation was the knowledge of certain truths concerning our lost condition, the love of God and the work of Christ. Similarly, the first steps in our spiritual growth came from other truths we learned from the Word of God. As we learn more truth, the Holy Spirit has more with which to work. Therefore, the more of God's Word we know, the greater our potential for growth.

Knowledge of the Word of God has certain beneficial effects in our lives. The opposite is also true. Ignorance of these truths will keep us from certain benefits. Here are some, but not all, of those benefits:

1. **Knowing the Word can give us understanding of the will of God.**

    "Wherefore, be ye not foolish,
    but understand
    what the will of the Lord is"
    (Ephesians 5:17 ASV).

    How do we know the will of God? The Word of God reveals the will of God! I have known people who claimed God talked personally to them. One man in New Jersey told me he did not need to read the Bible, for God talked to him directly, telling him what to do. The man's life was a total mess. While listening to this "voice" he made some very poor choices. Often the voice told my friend to do things that were contrary to what God had already revealed in his Word.

(Your thoughts, impressions and experiences)

*"This knowledge of the will of God will be the basis
for everything else the Holy Spirit is going to do within us."*

This misled soul did not know the true will of God. I talk with God every day. I talk to God in prayer and he talks back to me from his Word. I am careful never to say, "God told me" or "God said to me." Instead I say, "I felt God was saying to me" or "I believe God was impressing upon my mind." God always speaks from his Word.

If we are not in the Word of God, we will not know the will of God. We are foolish when we are ignorant of the Word of God. We are foolish because God gave us his Word to teach us what he wants us to know. This knowledge of the will of God will be the basis for everything else the Holy Spirit is going to do within us.

2. **Knowing the Word can cause our actions to be approved by God.**
Concerning our living for God, the Word teaches us to,

"Study to show thyself approved unto God, a workman that needeth not to be ashamed, rightly dividing the Word of truth"
(2 Timothy 2:15).

We are to study, or examine ourselves, in the light of the Word of God. The Word of God is the standard for judging our actions.

Experience has convinced me some Christians don't want to read their Bible because they don't want to hear what the Bible says about some things they are doing.

(Your thoughts, impressions and experiences)

*"The Scriptures lead us on to
spiritual maturity and equip us for service for God.*

People have told me they don't come to church anymore because they felt too much conviction about their lifestyle when they heard the Word of God being taught.

If we want to know what God wants of us today, we need to know what the Bible says. Then, when we go to the Word, we need to "rightly divide," or correctly handle, the Word. We must not confuse Israel's responsibility under the Mosaic law, with our responsibility under grace. We must make sure we understand the context so we know to whom God is talking. The entire Bible is written <u>for</u> us, but not all was written <u>to</u> us. Following the right marching orders will lead to actions approved by God.

3. **Knowing the Word can provide what is good for us.**
   God uses his Word to profit us in many ways.

   "All Scripture is God-breathed and is useful for teaching, rebuking, correcting and training in righteousness, so that the man of God may be thoroughly equipped for every good work"
   (2 Timothy 3:16-17 NIV).

From the Word of God we understand doctrine (teaching). The Word reproves and corrects us when we err and teaches us how to be righteous. The Scriptures lead us on to spiritual maturity and equip us for service for God.

(Your thoughts, impressions and experiences)

---

*"Faith believes God is who he says he is
and that he can and will do what he has promised."*

_____

_____

_____

_____

_____

_____

_____

_____

_____

_____

_____

_____

_____

_____

_____

_____

(Your thoughts, impressions and experiences)

In these two verses there are five ways we profit from the Word of God. How else could we know correct doctrine? How else could we know when we have sinned? How else could we be prepared for service? The Word of God provides all these benefits for us.

4. Knowing the Word can produce faith.

There is a great deal of confusion among believers concerning faith. What is faith? Faith is <u>not</u> telling God what we want him to do and then believing he will do it. This philosophy is not faith, it is presumption. For Abraham, faith was

> *"being fully
> persuaded that God
> had power
> to do what he
> had promised"*
> (Romans 4:21 NIV).

The same is true for us. Faith believes God is who he says he is and that he can and will do what he has promised. Notice, faith is based upon the promises of God, not the wants of man. Where do we find the promises of God? In the Word of God! Faith is based upon the Word,

> *"So then
> faith comes by hearing,
> and hearing by the
> Word of
> God"*
> (Romans 10:17 NKJV).

"There is no change in the believer's life apart from the Word of God. . . ."

How can we trust God to keep his promises, if we don't know who he is and what he has promised? We should be reading and studying the Word of God, if for no other reason than to know what we can trust God to do for us. When we placed our trust in him, we entered into a personal, eternal relationship with him based upon faith.

5. **Knowing the Word can change us.** There is no change in the believer's life apart from the Word of God;

> *"For this reason*
> *we also thank God*
> *without ceasing, because*
> *when you received the*
> *Word of God which*
> *you heard from*
> *us, you welcomed it*
> *not as the word of men,*
> *but as it is in truth,*
> *the word of God,*
> *which also effectively*
> *works in you who believe"*
> (1 Thessalonians 2:13 NKJV).

The work, which God's Word does within us, is changing us. There is no change without believing the Word and there is no believing without first knowing the Word. So if we don't know the Word, we will certainly never get to the point where the Word will change us.

An important part of this change is our deliverance from the power of sin in our lives. There is no deliverance apart from the Word.

(Your thoughts, impressions and experiences)

107

"When Satan tempted Jesus in the wilderness, Jesus always answered the temptation by quoting Scripture."

"Take heed unto thyself, and unto the doctrine; continue in them: for in doing this thou shalt both save thyself, and them that hear thee" (1 Timothy 4:16).

There are three tenses to our salvation: past, present and future. For all believers, God has saved us from the penalty of sin. Daily God is saving from the power of sin. Then someday, when we go to be with the Lord, he will save us from the presence of sin. Whenever we see the words "saved" or "salvation," we need to look at the context to discern its tense. First Timothy 4:16 is talking about being saved from the power of sin in our lives. This power comes from "taking heed to the doctrine." There is no way we can "take heed to the doctrine" if we don't know the doctrine. We must know the Word of God before it can bring us victory over sin.

6. **Knowing the Word can defeat Satan.**
God refers to his Word as

"the sword of the Spirit" (Ephesians 6:17).

The Word is said to be "Alive *and powerful*" (Hebrews 4:12).

When Satan tempted Jesus in the wilderness, Jesus always answered the temptation by quoting Scripture (Matthew 4:1-11).

(Your thoughts, impressions and experiences)

CHAPTER SIX
KNOW THE WORD OF GOD

"Satan has many ways to get us to neglect our "swords.""

Satan has tried repeatedly to keep people from reading the Bible. The Enemy of our souls has tried several times to destroy the Bible by having it banned or burned. When those tactics didn't work, the Devil used religion to keep people from reading the Bible. The church told the people, "Only the clergy can understand the Bible," and at one time the church prohibited the common people from reading God's Word.

But by far, Satan's best strategy is the one he is currently using. Satan's lie this time is that believers can neglect reading God's Word without any negative consequences. Many Christians go weeks, or even months, without ever opening their Bibles. The result of this neglect is they never grow in their walk with God.

Satan has many ways to get us to neglect our "swords." He keeps us so busy we do not have time to read or meditate on God's Word. Television numbs our minds with interesting distractions. We fill our time, which we could spend with God, collecting something. One especially good ploy of Satan's with the older crowd is to get them focused on travel and the pursuit of leisure time activities (called retirement).

Is it any wonder Satan wants to keep us out of the Bible? So much begins to happen when we read God's Word. With God's Word on a shelf, we are like a car without an engine.

(Your thoughts, impressions and experiences)

109

*"To aid us in our growth in
Bible knowledge, God created the church."*

We can look good, but we are powerless to move forward in our personal, intimate relationship with God.

The Importance of Going to a Bible-teaching Church

To aid us in our growth in Bible knowledge, God created the church. Why do we go to church? There are many answers to that question, but topping the list should be "to hear the Word of God taught." Paul told Timothy,

*"Preach the Word; be
prepared in season and
out of season; correct, rebuke
and encourage — with great patience
and careful instruction"*
(2 Timothy 4:2 NIV).

Timothy was a pastor. The primary responsibility of a pastor is to preach and teach the Word of God, allowing the Word to change people. Sad to say, the Word of God is almost totally ignored in some churches. Social commentary or gratuitous entertainment is often the norm. Storytellers have replaced preachers in the pulpit. Some pastors have forgotten, or never learned, that it is the Word of God that is alive, powerful and produces change in the believer's life.

Pastors are also supposed to be teaching future teachers.

*"And the things you have
heard me say in the presence of many
witnesses entrust to reliable men who
will also be qualified to teach others"*
(2 Timothy 2:2 NIV).

(Your thoughts, impressions and experiences)

> *"Not only is the pastor to teach the Word of God, but he is also to be reproducing himself in other reliable teachers."*

Not only is the pastor to teach the Word of God, but he is also to be reproducing himself in other reliable teachers. The pastor is to be a teacher of teachers. Paul describes a good minister as one who,

> *"puts the brethren*
> *in remembrance of*
> *these things"*
> (1 Timothy 4:6),

referring to the sound doctrine Paul taught Timothy.

God exhorts us to honor those pastors who faithfully proclaim the Word of God;

> *"Pastors who do*
> *their work*
> *well should be*
> *paid well*
> *and should be*
> *highly appreciated,*
> *especially those who*
> *work hard at both*
> *preaching and teaching"*
> (1 Timothy 5:17 TLB).

Sad to say, today churches often rate pastors on their administrative ability rather than on their ability to plainly teach the Word of God.

If the first element for spiritual growth is knowledge of the Word of God, and the primary job of the pastor is to preach and teach the Word, then believers need to be attending churches where the Bible is the center of all teaching.

(Your thoughts, impressions and experiences)

"[In the last days] demons will seduce believers away from the Word of God."

Last-day Prophecies Concerning the Word of God

Concerning the last days of the church (which can't be that far away), the apostle Paul wrote,

"The Spirit clearly says that in later times some will abandon the faith and follow deceiving spirits and things taught by demons"
(1 Timothy 4:1 NIV).

At that time demons will seduce believers away from the Word of God.

Something else will replace the Word. Perhaps the seduction will be some emotional experience, a religious "high." Perhaps it will be some philosophy that elevates man to be the controller of his life and "captain of his destiny." Whatever the seduction is, it will not be sound teaching from the Word of God.

Paul goes on to say,

"For the time will come when men will not put up with sound doctrine. Instead, to suit their own desires, they will gather around them a great number of teachers to say what their itching ears want to hear. They will turn their ears away from the truth and turn aside to myths"
(2 Timothy 4:3-4 NIV).

Christians will hate sound doctrine! Doctrine will become the enemy. They will say, "Doctrine is not practical and gets in the way of unity!"

(Your thoughts, impressions and experiences)

112

"The word 'can' speaks of potential, not certainty."

Or, "doctrine doesn't give us a warm, fuzzy feeling or an emotional high like music does. Let's have more singing and less preaching." The result, Paul says, is they are,

"always learning, but never able to come to the knowledge of the truth"
(2 Timothy 3:7).

There is a hunger to learn, but because they aren't interested in doctrine, they never see the truth. The Word cannot get into those who are not first in the Word.

WARNING!!!
Knowing the Word of God is the first element needed for spiritual growth, but it is only a first step. All of the six benefits of knowing the Word of God mentioned in this chapter contain the word "can," i.e., knowing the Word <u>can</u> provide what profits us. Knowing the Word <u>can</u> produce faith and facilitate an intimate relationship with God, etc. The word "can" speaks of potential, not certainty. We must mix this element with all of the other elements in order for the benefits to occur.

Knowledge alone is harmful to the believer;

"Knowledge puffs up, but love builds up"
(1 Corinthians 8:1 NIV).

Knowledge of God's Word can cause us to become proud. In chapter five we saw how pride keeps us from God's grace gifts. I have met many obnoxious Christians who were very proud of their knowledge of certain doctrines.

(Your thoughts, impressions and experiences)

113

*"Knowledge without love results
in our becoming judgmental and arrogant."*

For these Christians, knowledge of the truths of God's Word was the beginning and end of the Christian life. Using their Bible as a club, these vicious believers beat up on other Christians.

The apostle Paul knew a great deal of doctrine due to the abundance of revelations he received. Yet Paul said,

*If I have the gift of prophecy,
and can fathom all mysteries
and
all knowledge . . .
but have not love,
I am nothing"*
(1 Corinthians 13:2 NIV).

Knowledge without love results in our becoming judgmental and arrogant. It would be better, for Christ's sake and the sake of his church, that a person never learned anything of the Word of God than to learn just doctrine and stop there. At least this person would not be so offensive to those that need to come to Christ.

Speaking to the Jews who knew the Word of God but did not obey it, Paul warned,

*"God's name
is blasphemed among the Gentiles
because of you"*
(Romans 2:24 NIV).

The principle applies to us, too. When we know the Word of God but don't live it, we bring dishonor to God. We must have biblical knowledge, but we dare not stop there.

_____
_____
_____
_____
_____
_____
_____
_____
_____
_____
_____
_____
_____
_____

(Your thoughts, impressions and experiences)

CHAPTER SIX
KNOW THE WORD OF GOD

"Now it is our responsibility to pick up the Bible and start learning the truths God has for us."

Getting Into the Word of God

There is no spiritual growth apart from knowing the Word of God. God has done his part. By inspiration of the Holy Spirit He gave us the Word. Now it is our responsibility to pick up the Bible and start learning the truths God has for us. We can do this five ways.

1. Reading the Word

Set aside time each day for reading the Bible. Rather than starting at the beginning, Genesis, try starting with the Gospel of John or the book of Romans. I like Psalms because it speaks to my heart. I like Proverbs because it speaks to my mind. Jump around; enjoy the variety in the Bible. Read to gain knowledge of the truths of God's Word.

2. Studying the Word

Just as we set aside time to read the Bible, we also need to set aside time to study the Bible. A Bible study is more systematic, structured and organized than Bible reading. The two main Bible study methods are book studies and topical studies.

In book studies we take a book of the Bible and study it from beginning to end. This type of study helps us understand the context of truths and their relationship to other truths in God's Word. A topical study can jump all over the Bible, but always looking at one major theme. Your local Christian bookstore should have racks of good study books to help you study the Bible alone, or in small groups.

(Your thoughts, impressions and experiences)

"To develop intimacy with God we must meditate on the Word of God."

3. **Hearing the Word**

We have already talked about the importance of going to a Bible-teaching church. Let me just add, go often and go regularly. Take notes and put them in a notebook. Your pastor can be a tremendous source of information on the culture and background that is a part of the context of Scripture.

4. **Memorizing the Word**

When a verse or passage of Scripture is especially meaningful to you, take time to memorize it. When Satan tempted Christ in the wilderness, Christ did not have time to run home, grab his Bible and start looking for verses to throw back at him. We don't either. We need to memorize Scripture so we have it available to use when the need arises.

There are many Bible memorization programs available to us to help us memorize Scripture. I like the ones put out by the Navigators (NavPress). They follow specific themes so the student can memorize several verses that relate to each other. Knowledge without love results in our becoming judgmental and arrogant. Ask your pastor for some verses he would recommend.

5. **Meditating on the Word**

To develop intimacy with God we must meditate on the Word of God. Meditation is talking with God. We talk to him and he talks to us. I begin my meditation time by asking God to speak to me from his Word and show me what he has for me that day.

(Your thoughts, impressions and experiences)

"Meditation takes time and requires an uncluttered mind."

Then I open my Bible and start reading. Sometimes I read from a place I have in mind, and sometimes I feel God leading me to a particular passage he wants me to read. I read slowly, contemplating each verse for a few minutes until I come to a verse that seems to speak right to me. Then I meditate on that verse.

Meditation takes time and requires an uncluttered mind. Sometimes the busyness of my office makes it impossible to focus my mind. I have found some tranquil spots alone in the foothills of the Olympic Mountains or by a bay on Puget Sound that work for me. You need to find a spot or spots that will work for you, too.

DECISION TIME
No spiritual growth is possible without first knowledge from the Word of God. May I suggest a prayer something like this?

"God, I want to know
you and your word more.
Please give me the continued desire
and power to do the things necessary
to learn the truths of your Word."

Right now decide what you are going to do in terms of reading, studying, hearing, memorizing and meditating on the Word.

(Your thoughts, impressions and experiences)

CHAPTER SIX
QUESTIONS AND DISCUSSION

1. Why must Christians know the Word of God in order to grow in their walk with God?

   _____

   _____

   _____

   _____

2. List six benefits that begin with the knowledge of God's Word?
   a.
   b.
   c.
   d.
   e.
   f.

3. Which of these benefits is most significant to you right now? Why?

   _____

   _____

   _____

   _____

4. Why is it important to attend a Bible-teaching church?

   _____

   _____

   _____

   _____

   _____

5. What would you like to do in each of the following areas to improve your knowledge of God's word?

a. Reading the Word

_____

_____

_____

b. Studying the Word

_____

_____

_____

c. Hearing the Word

_____

_____

_____

d. Memorizing the Word

_____

_____

_____

e. Meditating on the Word

_____

_____

_____

PROJECT

Studying the Bible should never be replaced with studying about the Bible. If you are not already doing so, begin a Bible study. It can be a topical study or a book study. For new Christians, it is best to begin with a survey-type study rather than a deep study of a particular doctrine or biblical book. Your pastor or local Christian bookstore might recommend a good starting point for you. Get started right away.

ADDITIONAL JOURNALING

CHAPTER SEVEN
UNDERSTAND THE WORD OF GOD

"Knowledge of the Word of God is the first element needed for spiritual growth, but to knowledge we must add understanding."

In 2 Timothy 2:7 the apostle Paul told Timothy, *"Consider what I say, and may the Lord give you understanding in all things."* The word "understanding" here means to comprehend the meaning, value, importance and relevance of spiritual truth.

Understanding goes beyond knowledge. Many people believe Jesus lived and died, but do not understand how that knowledge is relevant to their lives today. These people know the information, but the value escapes them. God's Word tells us the Devil believes there is a God (James 2:19), but this knowledge has no value to him.

Knowledge of the Word of God is the first element needed for spiritual growth, but to knowledge we must add understanding. For example, it is not enough for us just to know God is omnipotent (all powerful).

We must also understand what relevance this doctrine has for us. Relevance will differ from person to person and situation to situation. We understand the relevance of the omnipotence of God as we specifically apply the doctrine to the different testings, trials and tribulations we endure.

For the family standing by the graveside of a believer, the relevance of God's omnipotence is in his promise and power to raise the dead. For the young pastor just going into the ministry, the relevance of the omnipotence of God may be in God's promise of power to do his work.

(Your thoughts, impressions and experiences)

"It is the Holy Spirit who reveals the meaning, importance, value and relevance of spiritual truth."

For the everyday homemaker or employee, the relevance of God's omnipotence may be in God's promise that his grace will be sufficient for each day.

So, how do we get the understanding? It is a free gift of God's grace! As we saw in 2 Timothy 2:7, the understanding comes from God. To be more specific, it is a result of the Holy Spirit working in our lives. In one of Paul's prayers for the Ephesians Paul prayed,

"That the God of our Lord Jesus Christ, the Father of glory, may give to you the spirit of wisdom and revelation in the knowledge of him, the eyes of your understanding being enlightened ..."
(Ephesians 1:17-18 NKJV).

It is the Holy Spirit who reveals the meaning, importance, value and relevance of spiritual truth.

Spiritual Growth and the Work of the Holy Spirit
The Holy Spirit's working within us is critical to our spiritual growth. It is the Holy Spirit's job to change us into the image of God.

"And we, who with unveiled faces all reflect the Lord's glory, are being transformed into his likeness with ever-increasing glory, which comes from the Lord, who is the Spirit"
(2 Corinthians 3:18 NIV).

We can't make ourselves more like God, but the Holy Spirit can.

(Your thoughts, impressions and experiences)

122

"What a list of rules and regulations can't do, the Holy Spirit can do, and that is to bring life to the believer."

Many books on Christian growth in my library say we grow as we do certain things. The books have lists of <u>do's</u> and <u>don'ts</u>, but God says that laws kill spiritual growth.

"For the letter kills, but the Spirit gives life"
(2 Corinthians 3:6 NIV).

The "letter that kills" refers to laws and lists of rules, the <u>do's</u> and <u>don'ts</u> of religion.

What a list of rules and regulations can't do, the Holy Spirit can do, and that is to bring life to the believer. The type of life mentioned in 2 Corinthians 3:6 is not the eternal life believers already possess. The life referred to here is the abundant life, the godlike life, a life characterized by godliness. One major reason God has given us his permanently indwelling Holy Spirit is to produce God's life within us.

The early church at Galatia thought Christian growth came through keeping certain religious rules and regulations. The actions of the Christians there shocked Paul, so he wrote,

"Are you so foolish? After beginning <u>with the Spirit</u>, are you now trying to attain your goal by human effort?"
(Galatians 3:3 NIV).

The goal to grow spiritually was right, but Paul rebuked them for not continuing the right way—with the Holy Spirit. Since the Holy Spirit brought them God's first free gift, eternal life, why couldn't they see the Holy Spirit would bring them God's other free gifts, too?

(Your thoughts, impressions and experiences)

"Man can know the truths of God's Word...but...
cannot understand truth...apart from the working of the Holy Spirit."

To these Galatians Paul wrote,

"But
by faith
we eagerly await
through the Spirit
the righteousness
for which we
hope"
(Galatians 5:5 NIV).

The righteousness spoken of here is not our position of righteousness or our right standing before God which, again, every believer already possesses. This righteousness is our day-by-day righteous living, including our desire to live godly and holy lives. The Holy Spirit within us makes it possible for us to do what is right.

"So I say,
live by the Spirit
and you will not gratify
the desires of the
sinful nature"
(Galatians 5:16 NIV).

The Holy Spirit Gives Us the Understanding.

Man can know the truths of God's Word by exercising his intellect, but man cannot understand truth (discern the meaning, value, relevance and importance) apart from the working of the Holy Spirit.

"There is
no one who understands,
no one who seeks
God"
(Romans 3:11 NIV).

(Your thoughts, impressions and experiences)

*"Were it not for the Holy Spirit
we would find God's truth absurd."*

Were it not for the Holy Spirit we would find God's truth absurd.

"The man without the Spirit does not accept the things that come from the Spirit of God, for they are <u>foolishness</u> to him, and he cannot understand them, because they are spiritually discerned"
(1 Corinthians 2:14 NIV).

It is impossible for our five physical senses to understand anything with a spiritual dimension. Spiritual understanding requires a "spiritual sense" which, in turn, requires the Holy Spirit's involvement.

"No eye has seen, no ear has heard, no mind has conceived what God has prepared for those who love Him, but God has <u>revealed it to us by His Spirit</u> . . . We have not received the spirit of the world but <u>the Spirit</u> who is from God, that we may <u>understand</u> what God has freely given us"
(1 Corinthians 2:9-10,12 NIV).

Logos and Rhema
There are two Greek words, found in the New Testament translated into one English word, "word." They are *logos* and *rhema*. Both of these Greek words have slightly different meanings, lost in the translation to English.

Logos is used more often than *rhema* in the New Testament. W.E. Vine in *The Expanded Vine's Expository Dictionary of New Testament Words* defines *logos* as: (a) embodying a concept or idea, (b) a saying or statement, (c) a discourse, speech or instruction.

(Your thoughts, impressions and experiences)

125

*"All of God's Word
is written for our instruction."*

The entire Bible is called the *logos* of God. All of the Bible is the expression of God's thoughts. All of God's Word is written for our instruction,

> "*All Scripture* is God-breathed and is useful for teaching, rebuking, correcting and training in righteousness" (2 Timothy 3:16).

Rhema has a little bit different meaning. W.E. Vine distinguishes the difference between *logos* and *rhema*;

> "The significance of *rhema* (as distinct from *logos*) is exemplified in the injunction to '*take the sword of the Spirit, which is the word of God,*' Eph. 6:17; here the reference is not to the whole Bible as such, but to the individual Scripture which the Spirit brings to our remembrance for use in time of need, a prerequisite being the regular storing of the mind with Scripture."

The entire Bible is the *logos* of God. When the Holy Spirit takes some part of the *logos* and reveals it to us during a time of need, thus showing us the relevance of God's Word, the passage becomes the *rhema* of God to us too. This *rhema* is what we are referring to in this chapter as understanding.

The *rhema* of God's Word brings us to a saving knowledge of Jesus Christ.

> "So then faith comes by hearing, and hearing by the word (rhema) of God" (Romans 10:17 NKJV).

(Your thoughts, impressions and experiences)

"We will not grow in our relationship with him unless we permit the Holy Spirit to continue his work within us to reveal and apply the Word to our lives."

Knowledge of Bible content alone does not bring us to faith. The working of the Holy Spirit through the Word of God, showing the value and relevance of biblical truth in our lives, reveals God's will to us and creates and sustains our faith.

We can know the Word (*logos*) of God but until we have the *rhema* (understanding the value, importance and relevance of his Word), we will not understand what God is doing or what he wants us to do. We will not grow in our relationship with him unless we permit the Holy Spirit to continue his work within us to reveal and apply the Word to our lives.

Having the Understanding Illustrated

Let us say we are reading in our Bibles and we come to Colossians 3:9,

"Do not lie to each other, since you have taken off your old self with its practices."
(Colossians 3:9 NIV),

Element One, knowing the Word, is fulfilled as we intellectually come to the realization that God does not want us to lie to one another. The Spirit-given understanding goes deeper than just knowing the truth. As we meditate on this truth, the Spirit might impress upon our minds that lying is morally wrong and a sin against God. Lying is an act of rebellion against God, for it goes against God's revealed will. We come to the understanding that God does not want us to lie to each other. Our conscience, having been made alive by the Holy Spirit, reveals to us where and when we lie.

(Your thoughts, impressions and experiences)

"Back then I was shocked to hear her say, 'I didn't think it mattered.' Today I am no longer surprised at the words or the attitude of indifference behind them."

Early in my ministry a woman came to me complaining about her unsaved husband. I asked her if she knew he was unsaved before she married him. She said, "Yes." I then asked her if she had known the Bible said we are not to be unequally yoked with unbelievers (2 Corinthians 6:14) before she married him. Again she responded, "Yes."

Unable to resist I asked her, "Then why did you marry him?" I was not ready for her answer. Looking me straight in the eyes, with sincerity written all over her face, she replied, "I didn't think it mattered." She knew what the Bible said, but she did not understand its importance, relevance, or value—so she disobeyed God.

Back then I was shocked to hear her say, "I didn't think it mattered." Today I am no longer surprised at the words or the attitude of indifference behind them.

In fact, I am convinced that many Christians are planning to repeat these words when they stand before God someday.

"I didn't think it mattered, so instead of loving my wife like Christ loved the church, I became a little dictator in my home." Or, "I didn't think it mattered, so I became bitter instead of forgiving others." Or, "I didn't think it mattered, so I committed adultery instead of being faithful to my spouse." Or, "I didn't think it mattered, so I gave nothing, or next to nothing, to support God's work." Or, "I didn't think it mattered, so I laid up all my treasures on earth instead of in heaven."

(Your thoughts, impressions and experiences)

CHAPTER SEVEN
UNDERSTAND THE WORD OF GOD

"Where there is no understanding of the Word, there is no reason to obey it."

I've got a news flash for all those who think it doesn't matter — IT DOES MATTER! If it is in God's Word, it matters. Otherwise it wouldn't be in the Bible! Thinking it doesn't matter is the primary evidence that we do not have an understanding of the Word. It is possible to know a great deal of doctrine, but not have the understanding of any of it.

Where there is no understanding of the Word, there is no reason to obey it. My wife and I have raised three children. As parents we know how critical it is that children obey because they understand the importance of doing so. We could force our children to obey us, but when we are no longer around, they will probably do as they wish.

When children truly understand the importance or value behind an action, they continue to act accordingly, even when the parents are no longer present. The same principle is true in applying our understanding of the Word to our daily lives. The Holy Spirit will not force us into obedience to God's Word or to the promptings of the Holy Spirit. It is up to us to apply the understanding that has been spiritually revealed to us.

Getting the Understanding
We have already seen it is the responsibility of the Holy Spirit to give us the understanding of God's Word. So why don't we have understanding automatically? The answer is that understanding is a gift received by faith similar to our salvation experience. Salvation is a free gift of God's grace, received by faith.

(Your thoughts, impressions and experiences)

"As a wise Father, God knows what we need, but he still wants us to ask."

Asking is an important part of receiving.

> *"You do not have*
> *because you do not ask*
> *God"*
> (James 4:2 NIV).

As a wise Father, God knows what we need, but he still wants us to ask. God's power can do more than we can imagine,

> *"Now to Him who*
> *is able to do immeasurably*
> *more than all we ask or*
> *imagine . . ."*
> (Ephesians 3:20 NIV).

Did you notice, though, implied is that God wants us to ask.

We do the asking in prayer. Praying for the Holy Spirit to reveal the value, relevance, importance and meaning of his Word in our lives, can be something we pray for ourselves and others. Paul prayed for believers,

> *"For this reason, since*
> *the day we heard about you,*
> *we have not stopped praying for you*
> *and asking God to fill you with the*
> *knowledge of His will through*
> *all spiritual wisdom and understanding"*
> (Colossians 1:9 NIV).

Through prayer we seek spiritual understanding and express our faith in God's Word to correctly direct our lives and the lives of those for whom we are praying.

(Your thoughts, impressions and experiences)

130

"While grieving the Holy Spirit deals more with sins of commission, quenching the Holy Spirit deals more with sins of omission."

Hindering the Holy Spirit

There are two things we can do that will definitely hinder the Holy Spirit's giving us spiritual insight and understanding: grieving and quenching the Holy Spirit.

We learn about grieving the Holy Spirit in Ephesians 4:30,

"And do not grieve the Holy Spirit..."
(Ephesians 4:30).

The context is a list of sins we might commit. We grieve the Holy Spirit when we do things that are wrong. Any parent can relate to this concept. Because we love our children, we feel hurt when they are naughty. The same is true of God.

We read about quenching the Holy Spirit in 1 Thessalonians 5:19,

"Do not quench the Spirit"
(1 Thessalonians 5:19 NKJ).

While grieving the Holy Spirit deals more with sins of commission, quenching the Holy Spirits deals more with sins of omission. When the Holy Spirit is trying to give spiritual understanding and we aren't listening, we are quenching the work of the Holy Spirit. We quench his work within us by refusing to do what he is prompting us to do. We quench the Holy Spirit by just not taking the time to listen to him.

Whenever we go to God's Word, God wants to speak to us.

(Your thoughts, impressions and experiences)

"By asking for his understanding, we are giving God the green light to reveal to us our sins and failings."

Not only does he want to teach us some truth, but he also wants to teach us the relevance, importance, value and meaning of that truth in our life. By asking for his understanding, we are giving God the green light to reveal to us our sins and failings. We are also telling him he may comfort us, encourage us or challenge us. Listening to a sermon may give us knowledge of God's Word, but whether or not that knowledge is translated into understanding is up to us. Sad to say, in many churches, when the sermon is over, people quickly scatter, forgetting the importance of what was said. I believe the most important ten minutes of church is the ten minutes after the message. It shouldn't be spent doing anything. It should be spent listening to God for "the understanding."

DECISION TIME

Have you been reading the Bible to gain information? That is good, but reading is not enough. Along with the knowledge must come the understanding and the wisdom of application. When you read the Bible, do you want to know its relevance, importance, value and meaning for your life?

Before you open the Bible to read, or before you listen to a sermon, may I suggest a prayer something like this:

"God, show me the importance and value of what I am going to see in your Word today. I want to understand, remember and apply to my life what your Holy Spirit is going to reveal to me."

(Your thoughts, impressions and experiences)

CHAPTER SEVEN
QUESTIONS AND DISCUSSION

1. Why is it important to understand the relevance of doctrine?

   _____

   _____

   _____

   _____

2. How do we obtain understanding?

   _____

   _____

   _____

   _____

3. Name three things the Holy Spirit is doing for us.

   _____

   _____

   _____

   _____

4. Define *logos*._____

   _____

   Define *rhema*._____

   _____

   Why is each important in our understanding God's will?_____

   _____

5. What is the significance of prayer in our understanding of what the Holy Spirit is instructing us to do through God's Word?

_____

_____

_____

_____

6. Identify ways in which you hinder or quench the work of the Holy Spirit in your life.

_____

_____

_____

_____

PROJECT

The purpose of Bible study is more than just the learning of Bible facts. Remember, we are building a deeper relationship with Christ. Therefore, no Bible study is complete until we understand the relevance, importance and value of what we have studied. As you study the Word of God, ask God for this understanding and then record it. Ask God for the ability to apply an understanding of his will to your life. When you share with other Christian friends what you have been learning from the Bible, be sure to share these personal insights, too.

_____

_____

_____

_____

_____

_____

CHAPTER EIGHT
BELIEVE THE WORD OF GOD

"[Abraham] staggered not at the promise of God through unbelief. . . ."

What does it mean to believe? Is belief an intellectual exercise or something we fabricate ourselves? If belief does not come from within us, then from where does belief come? In the New Testament, the English word "believe" is a translation of the Greek word "*pistos.*" The English word "faith" is also a translation of the same Greek word.

In Romans chapter four, within three verses the Greek word *pistos* is translated as both "faith" and "believed." Verse three states,

> "*Abraham
> believed God,
> and it was credited to him as
> righteousness*"
> (Romans 4:3).

Then in verse five we read,

> "*his faith
> is credited as
> righteousness*"
> (Romans 4:5).

So faith is believing God and believing God is faith. Using Abraham, we see faith illustrated in the same chapter.

> "*He staggered not at
> the promise of God
> through unbelief;
> but was strong in faith,
> giving glory to God;
> and being fully
> persuaded that,
> what he had promised,
> he was able also to perform*"
> (Romans 4:20-21).

(Your thoughts, impressions and experiences)

"Faith is not what we want to see happen,
but believing what God, through his Word has promised will happen."

Faith is a confidence that God can and will keep his promises. The object of our faith is God. His ability to do what he said he would do is the basis for our faith.

Our belief in God's ability and consistency is truly different from what some people claim faith to be. There are those who would have us believe that faith is our telling God what we want him to do, and then believing he will do it. That is not faith, it is presumption! Faith is not what we want to see happen, but believing what God, through his Word has promised will happen.

The Importance of Faith
How important is it that we believe God? Consider these statements from the Word of God.

"Everything that does not come from
faith is <u>sin</u>"
(Romans 14:23 NIV).

"And without faith it is <u>impossible</u> to please God"
(Hebrews 11:6 NIV).

Without faith we would never have received God's first gift, eternal life. Also, without faith we will never receive the rest of God's free gifts.

Speaking of Israel's years of wandering in the wilderness we read,

"But the message they heard was of <u>no value</u> to them, because those who heard did not combine it with faith"
(Hebrews 4:2 NIV).

(Your thoughts, impressions and experiences)

"Not believing God is not trusting God, and not trusting God is sin."

God told the children of Israel what he wanted them to do. God explained the relevance and value of obeying him. But because Israel did not mix the truth with faith, the truth was of no value to them.

Israel's lack of faith kept them from entering the Promised Land,

*"So we see
that
they were not
able to enter,
because of their
unbelief"*
(Hebrews 3:19 NIV).

All of the adults except Caleb and Joshua who left Egypt died before entering the Promised Land. They could not please God because their actions were not a result of faith. The writer of Hebrews has an application for us today.

*"See to it, brothers,
that
none of you
has
a sinful, unbelieving heart
that
turns away from
the living God"*
(Hebrews 3:12 NIV).

Not believing God is not trusting God, and not trusting God is sin. The original sin in the Garden of Eden was not believing God. First Satan cast doubt on what God said and then he proclaimed God to be a liar. "If God cannot be trusted, then why obey Him?" is Satan's underlying message to Eve.

(Your thoughts, impressions and experiences)

"Without faith we will not obey God."

"... 'Did God really say, "You must not eat from any tree in the garden"?' The woman said to the serpent, 'We may eat fruit from the trees in the garden, but God did say, "You must not eat fruit from the tree that is in the middle of the garden, and you must not touch it, or you will die." 'You will not surely die,' the serpent said to the woman. 'For God knows that when you eat of it your eyes will be opened, and you will be like God, knowing good and evil...'"
(Genesis 3:1-5 NIV).

When Eve, then Adam ate of the forbidden fruit, they were giving testimony they no longer believed God, but now believed Satan. Friends, Satan has not changed his approach. He does not want us to believe God. Without faith we will not obey God. Without faith we have no reason to believe God. Faith is the basic foundation of our relationship with the Father. That is why

"Without faith it is impossible to please God"
(Hebrews 11:6).

What Believing Does for Me –and You
The same gifts that come to us by the grace of God (chapter one) are also products of the Word of God (chapter five). These gifts are the result of faith and the three elements, knowing, understanding and believing God's Word, working together to make God's promises a reality in our lives. Our faith response (believing God) directed toward the promises found in the Word of God, come to us by the grace of God.

(Your thoughts, impressions and experiences)

CHAPTER EIGHT
BELIEVE THE WORD OF GOD

"Faith is the basic foundation of our relationship with the Father."

If we were to ask three people where we get water, we might get three different answers, all of which could be true. One might say, "We get it from a reservoir in the mountains." Another might say, "It comes from the pipes under the street." A third might say, "It comes from the faucet in the kitchen." All three are right and all three sources are necessary to get the water.

If we ask three Christians what saves us, we might also get three answers, and they could all be correct. One might say, "We are saved by the grace of God." Another might say, "It is the Word of God that brings us salvation." The third might say, "It is faith." All three are right! All three are necessary!

Faith is one of the elements necessary for salvation.

*"For it is by grace
you have been saved,
through faith"*
(Ephesians 2:8 NIV).

Faith is the only authorized response to God's grace. In what is probably the best-known verse in Scripture we read,

*"For God so loved
the world,
that he gave his
only begotten Son,
that
whosoever believeth in him
should not perish,
but have everlasting
life"*
(John 3:16).

(Your thoughts, impressions and experiences)

139

"A lack of confidence in God will always rob us of our peace."

Salvation, through Christ Jesus, comes to them that believe.

In similar fashion, believing God brings us all the rest of God's free gifts.

"Now the God of hope fill you with all joy and peace in __believing__"
(Romans 15:13).

Notice the condition for our being filled with joy and peace. It is believing! If we have an absence of joy and peace in our life, the solution is to start believing the promises of God. A lack of faith in God robs us of our joy. A lack of confidence in God will always rob us of our peace.

Our belief is also a condition for receiving God's power. That we might experience

"his incomparably great power for __us who believe__. That power is like the working of his mighty strength"
(Ephesians 1:19 NIV).

There is no divine power without faith. Power for victory over sin, power for fruitful service and power to forgive are all a result of believing God.

Sometimes we pray for God's power to deal with some problem in our life and are confused and dismayed because the problem doesn't go away. We don't understand that power comes as a result of our believing God. When we are trusting ourselves and our own abilities, we cannot be trusting God. So God withholds his power to bring us to the point where we have no choice but to trust him.

(Your thoughts, impressions and experiences)

CHAPTER EIGHT
BELIEVE THE WORD OF GOD

"We must also believe the Word of God or it cannot bring us forward toward spiritual maturity."

How much easier it would be if we just started out believing him.

Faith also allows the Word of God to do its work within us.

"When you received the word of God, . . .you accepted it not as the word of men, but as it actually is, the word of God, which is at work in you who believe"
(1 Thessalonians 2:13 NIV).

Without faith, God's Word cannot do anything. We are like the children of Israel who did not profit from the Word of God because they did not mix it with faith.

Knowing the Word is not enough. Understanding the value, relevance and importance of the Word is not enough. We must also believe the Word of God or it cannot bring us forward toward spiritual maturity.

The Only Other Options
Everybody believes something, so the choice is not if we will believe, but who or what we will believe. Some people choose to believe their circumstances. For them the circumstances of life become more real than the promises of God.

The apostle Peter learned that believing in one's circumstances is a real "letdown." Jesus sent the disciples on ahead of him in a boat to cross over to the other side of the Sea of Galilee. Jesus said he would join them later, and join them he did, but in a most unusual manner.

(Your thoughts, impressions and experiences)

"God never intended for us to live under negative circumstances, he wants us to live above them."

Jesus walked on top of the water and met the boat in the middle of the sea. At first the disciples were frightened at the sight, but upon realizing it was Jesus they calmed down—all but Peter. Peter got really excited and asked Jesus,

"Lord if it is you...tell me to come to you on the water"
(Matthew 14:28).

The Lord said, "come" and Peter got out of the boat and walked on the water to Jesus. At the beginning of his walk, Peter's faith was in Jesus. And then we read,

"But when he looked around at the high waves, he was terrified and began to sink. 'Save me, Lord!' he shouted"
(Matthew 14:30 TLB).

Peter took his eyes off Christ and placed them on his circumstances. His circumstances, the waves, became more real to Peter than our Lord's command to walk on the water. At the moment of unbelief, Peter began to sink.

If we don't believe God, then we will believe our circumstances. Then when the circumstances of life become overwhelming, we will sink in despair beneath them. Occasionally I will ask people how they are doing and they respond "Fairly well, under the circumstances." I always want to come back with, "What are you doing <u>under</u> the circumstances?" God never intended for us to live under negative circumstances, he wants us to live above them.

(Your thoughts, impressions and experiences)

CHAPTER EIGHT
BELIEVE THE WORD OF GOD

"There are going to be times when what God asks us to believe and what we think is logical are going to clash."

Living under the circumstances is a dead giveaway that people are believing what they perceive with their five physical senses instead of what God has promised.

The wisest man who ever lived, Solomon, admonished people to,

"Trust in the Lord with all your heart and lean not on your own understanding; in all your ways acknowledge him, and he will make your paths straight. Do not be wise in your own eyes"
(Proverbs 3:5-7 NIV).

There are going to be times when what God asks us to believe and what we think is logical are going to clash. All of our circumstances are pointing in one direction but God is pointing in the opposite direction. At those times we are to totally disregard what seems right to us and totally trust what God says.

When we choose to believe our circumstances instead of God, what we are really telling God is that we know better than he does. Therefore, we will follow what we think is best instead of what God says. This is a sure evidence of pride. God said,

"As the heavens are higher than the earth, so are my ways higher than your ways, and my thoughts than your thoughts"
(Isaiah 55:9 NIV).

When this truth gets a hold of us, we will believe God instead of our circumstances.

(Your thoughts, impressions and experiences)

"As we see his power, love and faithfulness, as revealed in his Word, our faith in God increases."

Getting More Faith

There is no secret for having more faith. God has told us,

*"So then faith
cometh by hearing,
and hearing
by
the Word of God"*
(Romans 10:17).

It is hard to believe and trust someone we hardly know. But the more we get to know them, the more we know whether they are trustworthy. The same is true with God. As we see his power, love and faithfulness, as revealed in his Word, our faith in God increases. As we see him keep his promises to us, found in his Word, we will trust God more.

When a man brought his demon possessed son to Jesus for healing, Jesus told the man to have faith and his son would be healed. The father replied,

*"I do have faith; oh,
help me to have more!"*
(Mark 9:24 TLB).

What a good prayer for us! When we open the Word of God we need to pray, "Lord, show me truths that will increase my faith." Perhaps he will lead us to a passage that will indicate that he, and he alone, is worthy of our trust. Perhaps the passage will remind us of his power, love, goodness or faithfulness. Or perhaps God's Word will show us the futility of trusting in our circumstances or ourselves. God has many ways of answering a prayer for a stronger faith.

(Your thoughts, impressions and experiences)

144

"Part of our prayers for others should be that they too might take up the shield of faith (believe God)."

While we are praying for more faith for ourselves, why not pray the same prayer for others? In our battle against Satan, God's Word tells us to

"take up the shield of faith,
with which you can extinguish
all the flaming arrows
of the evil one"
(Ephesians 6:16 NIV).

Then, getting to the actual warfare we read,

"with this in mind,
be alert and always
keep on praying for
all the
saints"
(Ephesians 6:18 NIV).

Part of our prayers for others should be that they too might take up the shield of faith (believe God).

Knowing, Understanding and Believing Illustrated

When I need to purchase airline tickets, I always go to my local travel agent. She does something that illustrates the difference between knowing, understanding and believing a truth.

She sits at her computer and punches in some keystrokes and information appears on her monitor. Now, she has been to travel agent school and knows what the symbols on her monitor mean. She has the knowledge necessary to process the wealth of information at her disposal; meaningless information until a customer comes in with a particular request.

(Your thoughts, impressions and experiences)

"God has never failed anyone yet."

The information has value or relevance only when a customer wants to fly from one place to another. Flights, times, connections and fares are no longer just abstract tidbits of information but now take on meaning which the travel agent understands.

The agent must also have faith. She must believe the information is reliable or trustworthy. If in the past she has found that the information displayed on the monitor to be inaccurate, she might not want to believe what she is reading. But if her experience with the program has always been positive, then she would not hesitate to believe what she sees displayed before her.

Until we come to God with a need, all the information found in the Bible is just so much head knowledge. When we come to God's Word seeking to understand how it relates to our personal needs, the Holy Spirit shows us the relevance, importance and value of God's message. Without faith, we will never believe God. If we don't believe God, then we won't act upon what we know from his Word.

God has never failed anyone yet. He is completely trustworthy, now we must choose to believe him. It would be a complete waste of time for a travel agent to go to school to learn how to do the job, but not believe the information displayed on the screen. If she didn't believe the information, she would never act upon it. It is the same with Christians. It is a total waste of time to learn how to live the Christian life if we don't believe God.

(Your thoughts, impressions and experiences)

146

CHAPTER EIGHT
BELIEVE THE WORD OF GOD

"Believing is more an act of the will than an act of the intellect."

We will never act upon what we know until we believe God's truth found in his Word.

DECISION TIME

Believing is more an act of the will than an act of the intellect. We believe what we choose to believe. In deciding what we want to believe, we draw heavily from previous experiences. If a certain chair has always held my weight, I will choose to believe I can safely sit on it. If the lights always come on when I push a certain button, and I want the lights to go on again, I will push the same button.

Do you believe God saved you when you put your trust in Christ? If so, do you believe God can do other things for you when you put your trust in him? Has God ever failed to keep a promise to you or anyone else? Perhaps a good prayer today might be, "God, thank you for keeping your promises. I commit myself to believing you, even if it goes against my own understanding."

(Your thoughts, impressions and experiences)

CHAPTER EIGHT
QUESTIONS AND DISCUSSION

1. Define faith and discuss how we associate faith with our understanding of and our relationship with God.

   _____

   _____

   _____

   _____

2. How important to you is your belief in God? In your journal list ways in which you express your belief and trust in God.

   _____

   _____

   _____

   _____

3. Refer to chapter one's discussion of God's free gifts that come to us by grace. Reflect on the connection between the expressions of your faith listed in question two and the resulting gifts from God that you have received through your faith. Discuss this connection in your journal.

   _____

   _____

   _____

   _____

4. What is the condition for our being filled with joy and peace? What is the solution for an absence of joy and peace in our lives?

   _____

   _____

5. What is the true source of spiritual power in our lives?

_____

_____

_____

_____

6. Why is knowing the Word and understanding the value, relevance and importance of the Word not enough for Christians?

_____

_____

_____

_____

7. How can you increase your faith?

_____

_____

_____

_____

PROJECT
Make a list of instances when God fulfilled his promises to you. Update this list on an ongoing basis and share it with others.

_____

_____

_____

_____

_____

ADDITIONAL JOURNALING

CHAPTER NINE
DESIRE TO OBEY THE WORD OF GOD

"How important is desire?"

How important is desire? Ken Kemper, a former missionary to Tanzania, tells this story concerning the power of desire. When the natives go out to catch monkeys, they use the monkey's own desire as a trap. It seems that monkeys love peeled oranges. So the natives cut a coconut in half, hollow it out and place a peeled orange inside. They tie the two halves together and cut a hole into the side of the coconut. The hole is just big enough for a monkey to put his hand through, but not big enough to get the orange out. The coconut is then attached to a tree with vines.

When a monkey comes along, it smells the orange and places its hand inside the coconut to get the much-desired fruit. At this time the natives rush and capture the monkey. Now the monkey has a decision to make. It can either let go of the orange and flee to safety, or it can stay there, hanging on to the orange. Inevitably the monkey will scream and jump up and down, but won't let go of the orange. The result is the monkey is caught and eaten for dinner. The **desire** for the orange is so strong that it overrules the warning from the mind to flee when an enemy approaches.

Recently, just for fun, I attended one of those success and motivational seminars. In the first session the speaker shared the three elements necessary for success.

The three elements are:
1. Natural abilities and talents,
2. Knowledge/education/training,
3. Desire to succeed

(Your thoughts, impressions and experiences)

"The desire to receive God's blessings is important to the process of growing in godliness."

All of our abilities and education will not produce success until we have desire. One of the speaker's favorite sayings was, "Your attitude determines your altitude." To a certain extent I believe this is true. Without a desire for salvation none of us would be saved.

I don't know about you, but when I got saved the speaker presented the facts concerning salvation and then said something like this, "Now if you would like to become a Christian, have your sins forgiven and receive God's gift of eternal life, here is what you must pray...." Those words, "if you would like" speak of the desire to become a child of God. Until that desire is there, no one prays to be saved.

To be more specific, first came the knowledge,

"How shall they believe in him of whom they have not heard?"
(Romans 10:14 NKJV).

Second, the Holy Spirit brought the understanding—discerning the value, importance and relevance of what we heard. Third, we believed that what we heard was true— God can and will save us. Fourth, and the point of this chapter, we desired to be saved. If there was no desire, there was no continuation of the process that leads to salvation.

DESIRING THE PROCESS
The desire to receive God's blessings is important to the process of growing in godliness.

(Your thoughts, impressions and experiences)

CHAPTER NINE
DESIRE TO OBEY THE WORD OF GOD

" One reason we don't ask is that we don't really desire <u>all</u> that God wants for us."

*J*ames tells us,

"You have not, because you ask not"
(James 4:2).

But why don't we ask? One reason we don't ask is that we don't really desire <u>all</u> that God wants for us.

I struggled with this idea at first. For instance, I had prayed, occasionally, for God to fill me with his love. I told him I wanted to feel his love in my life. Yet, I was disappointed. I thought I had the desire, but I wasn't getting the love for which I asked.

Later I discovered the reason I didn't experience God's unconditional love in my life. As I was preparing a message to preach for a Sunday night service, the Lord spoke to me from his Word. This is the passage I read,

"We can rejoice, too, when we run into problems and trials, for we know that they are good for us— they help us learn to be patient. And patience develops strength of character in us and helps us trust God more each time we use it until finally our hope and faith are strong and steady. Then, when that happens, we are able to hold our heads high no matter what happens and know that all is well, for we know how dearly God loves us, and <u>we feel this warm love everywhere within us because God has given us the Holy Spirit to fill our hearts with his love</u>"
(Romans 5:3-5 TLB).

_____

_____

_____

_____

_____

_____

_____

_____

_____

_____

_____

_____

_____

_____

_____

(Your thoughts, impressions and experiences)

153

"God wants us to desire the whole package he has planned for us, including the trials and tribulations."

I believed God was saying to me there is a process that leads to God filling me with his warm love. The process begins with problems and trials. As we believe that God is going to use them for good in our lives (Romans 8:28), we learn patience, or endurance. As our faith grows, we learn to trust God more and then, as we see he is always faithful to us, we understand how much he loves us. The result is that we experience his love in our lives. This is all a result of the Holy Spirit at work within us.

Where does <u>desire</u> fit into all of this? I desired the result and was disappointed when I didn't experience it. God was telling me that day I should desire the process needed to produce the result. It is not enough to just know the verse where God has promised to

"Work all things together for good to those that love him..."
(Romans 8:28).

I must understand the verse applies to me and believe that God can and will keep this promise. Then I must desire <u>the process</u> as much as the result. God wants us to desire the whole package he has planned for us, including the trials and tribulations.

Besides love, God gives many other grace gifts in trials and tribulations. For example:

Peace - Peace is not found in the absence of trials or tribulations. Peace is something God desires to give us in the midst of our problems.

(Your thoughts, impressions and experiences)

CHAPTER NINE
DESIRE TO OBEY THE WORD OF GOD

"Joy is different from happiness."

"Do not be anxious about anything, but in everything, by prayer and petition, with thanksgiving, present your requests to God. And the peace of God, which transcends all understanding, will guard your hearts and your minds in Christ Jesus" (Philippians 4:6-7 NIV).

The admonition not to be anxious implies that there is something to be anxious about. There is a trial or tribulation in our life. However, there is also the promise of peace while going through the problem.

Joy - Joy is different from happiness. Happiness is dependent upon our specific circumstances moment to moment. When things are going well, we are happy. When things aren't going well, we lose our happiness. Joy is different. Joy is the deeper, more profound, awareness that comes from God and is another one of his grace gifts that can come to us in times of tribulation. The apostle Paul prayed for the Colossians' growth

"... being strengthened with all power according to his glorious might so that you may have great endurance and patience, and *joyfully giving thanks* to the Father..." (Colossians 1:11-12 NIV).

Again, words like "strengthened, endurance and patience" imply there is some problem being experienced by the believer. But in the midst of the problem, the believer is joyfully giving thanks to God. Joy is the result.

(Your thoughts, impressions and experiences)

155

"Paul desired the trials and tribulations, knowing they would produce the power of God in his life."

The process needed to get the joy is dependent upon, and the result of, the testings and afflictions.

Love, joy and peace are the *"fruit of the Spirit"* (Galatians 5:22) and as such are gifts of God given by the Holy Spirit. They are gifts, yet we have seen these three virtues are connected to problems in our life. The question for us now is, "How much do we desire these virtues in our life?" Do we desire them enough to desire the process needed to produce them? The apostle Paul claimed,

"Therefore I will boast all the more gladly about my weaknesses, so that Christ's power may rest upon me. That is why, for Christ's sake, I delight in weaknesses, in insults, in hardships, in persecutions, in difficulties..."
(2 Corinthians 12:9-10 NIV).

Paul desired the trials and tribulations, knowing they would produce the power of God in his life. Without the desire to go through the process, Paul would have been just another whining Christian complaining about all the unfair things that happened to him.

WHERE DOES THE DESIRE COME FROM?

Perhaps you are sitting there in your easy-chair saying, "But I don't desire to go through life's weaknesses, insults, hardships, persecutions and difficulties. I know I should, and I see the importance of it in receiving many of God's blessings, but I just don't want to go through the process to get the result." Well, welcome to the human race!

(Your thoughts, impressions and experiences)

CHAPTER NINE
DESIRE TO OBEY THE WORD OF GOD

> *"God says he will give us the desire to submit to the process of receiving his blessings."*

I have always put great stock in the motto: "Pain hurts." And I, for one, go to great ends to eliminate pain from my life. I even gave up pizzas for a couple months, because the doctor said cheese (and other dairy products) might be causing my kidney stones. But again, God has the answer to our problem. God says he will give us the desire to submit to the process of receiving his blessings.

> *"For it is God who works in you to will and to act according to his good purpose"*
> (Philippians 2:13 NIV).

The word "will" here is translated from the Greek word that means, "to will, delight in or desire." The same Greek word is translated "desire" in Matthew 16:24-25 in the New King James Version,

> *"Then Jesus said to his disciples, 'If anyone desires to come after me, let him deny himself, and take up his cross, and follow me.*
> *For whoever desires to save his life shall lose it,*
> *but whoever loses his life for my sake shall find it."*
> (Matthew 16:24-25).

Philippians 2:13 tells us where this desire originates. God wants to put the desire in us to do all for his good pleasure. This is another work of the Holy Spirit. In chapter six we saw the Holy Spirit give us the understanding, and now we see the Holy Spirit giving us the desire to do the will of God. The same conditions and hindrances we looked at in chapter six apply here too.

(Your thoughts, impressions and experiences)

"We need to ask God for the desire and not quench or grieve the Holy Spirit."

We need to ask God for the desire and not quench or grieve the Holy Spirit, hindering him from working in our lives. For a review on how we quench or grieve the Holy Spirit, reread chapter six.

HOW ALL THIS APPLIES TO MY CHRISTIAN LIFE

I belong to two groups of people who constantly ignore the principle that desire must come before obedience. They are pastors and parents. As both a pastor and a parent, I am concerned about people obeying God. I want my children to obey God so they will have a life full of fruitful service for him. As they are obeying God, they will also obey my wife and me as the God-given authority in the home.

As a pastor I want the congregation to obey God for the same reasons. I want their lives to be full of the things the Holy Spirit can give them. As a side benefit there would be no power struggles anywhere in the church. The church would be a great testimony to the world and the unsaved as they witness authentic Christianity at work.

But what happens when someone in the family or in the church is disobedient to God? In some churches and Christian schools individuals are kicked out. Disobedience is an act of the will, and the individual who chooses to disobey is no longer worthy of being part of the assembly. I have seen the same thing happen in homes. A wayward child is dead to the parents. They are "out" with no chance of ever getting back "in" again.

(Your thoughts, impressions and experiences)

CHAPTER NINE
DESIRE TO OBEY THE WORD OF GOD

"We all know more than we put into practice in our lives."

Not every Christian school, church or family operates in such a cold fashion. Some see disobedience as an act of the intellect and will. Before they kick out the disobedient individual, the leadership wants to know if the person knew it was wrong to commit the act. If the offender can convince the leadership the sin was done in *"ignorance and unbelief"* one can obtain mercy (1 Timothy 1:13). On the other hand, if the offender knew what the Bible said about the matter and was disobedient anyway, well then, the sinner is dismissed from the church. The rationale here is that if someone knows something is wrong, then committing it is a sin and sin must be punished.

The trouble is, we all know more than we put into practice in our lives. Do our eating habits always reflect our knowledge of nutrition? Most of us know we should eat better, but choose to be inconsistent in our eating habits. Does our daily activity reflect our knowledge of proper exercise? How many of us have said, "I need to get more exercise"? But have we done it? Most of the time I haven't. How many Christians have said, "I need to pray more...read the Bible more...attend church more..."? Why is there such a large gap between what we know and what we do? I believe it is because we are missing the whole idea of "desire."

We assume if people know they should do the right thing, they will do it. When they don't, we get upset. We ask our children, "Why did you do that?" The answer we get back is either a shrug of the shoulders or mumble, "I don't know."

(Your thoughts, impressions and experiences)

159

"When our intellect and desires conflict, we usually obey our desires."

The correct answer is "I did it because I <u>wanted</u> to do it." When our intellect and desires conflict, we usually obey our desires. Every used car salesman knows this truth! When our mouth says we want a practical car, but our eyes can't conceal a desire for a sports car, the salesman will push the sports car every time, usually making the sale. Simi-larly, when our knowledge of what the Bible says we should do and our desires conflict, we will often follow the leading of our desires. Until we desire to obey God's Word, our obedience will not be our first choice.

So as pastors or parents, how do we help those under our authority to be obedient to God? One thing we can do is to understand that the connecting element between the intellect and behavior is desire. Once we understand this we can teach others the concept of obedience based upon desire. We can teach the importance of having godly desires. And we can teach that God wants to give those desires to us. We can pray for ourselves, seeking the desire to do the will of God. We can pray that we might desire to be active in the process, not just seeking the results. Then we can pray this prayer for others.

When counseling those who have been disobedient to God, we can share the need for desiring to obey God. We can stress the importance of yielding to the Holy Spirit and not quenching his leading, so that the Holy Spirit is free to continue his work within us, including giving us the desire to do the will of God.

(Your thoughts, impressions and experiences)

CHAPTER NINE
DESIRE TO OBEY THE WORD OF GOD

"The desire to do the complete will of God comes from the working of the Holy Spirit."

DECISION TIME

Take a few minutes to evaluate your desire to obey God. Are there areas in your life where you are disobedient to God? What is your true desire in these areas? Are you willing to ask God to change your desires? Also, evaluate your desire to go through the process, often including trials and tribulations, which will, in the end, result in more of God's blessings. Do you desire to be all that God wants you to be even if it involves personal pain?

Remember the desire to do the complete will of God comes from the working of the Holy Spirit. Is there anything in your life that is grieving or quenching the Holy Spirit's work within you? Perhaps the flesh is so strongly in control of your life that you don't even want to desire to obey God. If this is true, go back and read chapter one again. Remind yourself of what we miss when we say "no" to the rest of God's free gifts.

_____

_____

_____

_____

_____

_____

_____

_____

_____

(Your thoughts, impressions and experiences)

CHAPTER NINE
QUESTIONS AND DISCUSSION

1. What are some character traits or virtues you desire in your life?

   _____

   _____

   _____

   _____

2. What hinders you from having these traits?

   _____

   _____

   _____

   _____

3. Write a paragraph telling God you desire the process as well as the result of developing these character traits.

   _____

   _____

   _____

   _____

4. In what area of your life do you find your desires to obey God the weakest?

   _____

   _____

   _____

   _____

5. Write a prayer to God asking him to increase your desire for obedience in this weak area.

_____

_____

_____

6. Examine your life for any areas where you are grieving or quenching the Holy Spirit. Ask God to reveal these sins to you.

_____

_____

_____

7. Write a paragraph asking God for the desire and power to have victory over these sinful areas. Search your Bible for at least one reference for each area.

_____

_____

_____

PROJECT
List the areas in your life where you are disobedient to God or where you are not listening to the Holy Spirit's working within you to bring about positive change. Reflect upon each area, praying for guidance and God's grace.

_____

_____

_____

_____

ADDITIONAL JOURNALING

CHAPTER TEN
EMPOWERED TO OBEY THE WORD OF GOD

"We have no excuses for disobeying God."

I remember the day well. I had been reading a devotional booklet and the thought for the day was, "God never asks us to do anything we can't do." The point the writer was making was that we have no excuses for disobeying God. We can't whine, "I can't!" like a small child. As I was meditating on this thought, I had the opposite thought, "God never asks me to do anything I can do."

Desiring to do something and having the power to do it are two different things. We could desire to compose music like Bach, and even have volumes of his music to study, and be unable to create wonderful music. We could desire to paint like Rembrandt, have copies of his paintings, but still couldn't paint anything inspirational. Likewise, we can desire to do the will of God, and even have great examples to look at in the Bible or in our church, but still lack the power to do his will.

In chapter two we saw that the flesh has no power to do the will of God. Just this past week a young man shared his frustration with me. "*I don't want to go out drinking. Even while I am driving to the bar I am saying to myself that I don't want to do this, but I do it anyway.*" The apostle Paul looked into his own life and said,

> *"I do not understand*
> *what I do.*
> *For what I want to do*
> *I do not do,*
> *but what I hate I do"*
> (Romans 7:15 NIV).

(Your thoughts, impressions and experiences)

"We don't have the power because God's plan for us is to be weak, helpless and unable to do anything to make ourselves better."

The desire to do good was there, but the power to accomplish goodness was missing. Everyone who has tried to have daily devotions and failed knows this frustration. Anyone who has tried to have victory over a sinful habit, or made a promise to God to be a better person, only to find himself or herself the same old person a few months later, knows there is a Grand Canyon between the desire and the power to obey God.

Why don't we have the power? We don't have the power because God's plan for us is to be weak, helpless and unable to do anything to make ourselves better.

*"Not that
we are competent
in ourselves to claim anything
for ourselves, but our competence
comes from
God"*
(2 Corinthians 3:5 NIV).

God has put this void in our lives to draw us to him, so he might give us his power. Our weakness drives us to despair and then to God for the answer.

*"O unhappy and pitiable
and wretched man that I am! Who will
release and deliver me from the
shackles of this body of death?
O thank God! He will!
Through Jesus Christ,
the Anointed One, our Lord!
So then indeed I of myself with the
mind and heart serve the Law of God,
but with the flesh
the law of sin"*
(Romans 7:24-25 AMP).

(Your thoughts, impressions and experiences)

166

CHAPTER TEN
EMPOWERED TO OBEY THE WORD OF GOD

"God, within us in the person of the Holy Spirit, energizes us."

Paul came to the end of his rope and was ready to give up. In that place of weakness and despair, he found God's power to continue forward when he couldn't move under his own power.

THE POWER COMES FROM GOD
The same verse that tells us from where the desire comes also tells us from where the power comes.

"For it is God who works in you both to will and to do for His good pleasure" (Philippians 2:13 NKJV).

The words "to do" come from one Greek word, *energeo*, the same word from which we get our English word "energy." It means "to be at work within" or "to energize from within."

We have all seen the television commercial featuring the pink bunny beating on a drum. The battery **energizes** the bunny and gives it the power to keep going. Likewise, God, within us in the person of the Holy Spirit, energizes us. What would happen to the pink bunny if, for some reason, the battery became inoperative? Would it still have the power to keep working? No, the bunny is useless without the power supplied by the battery. In the same way, when the Holy Spirit becomes inoperative in our lives, we do not have the supernatural power of God to obey him.

Why did God choose to operate this way? Speaking of God's life within us as a special treasure, the apostle Paul puts it this way,

(Your thoughts, impressions and experiences)

"If we could live the Christian life by our own power, then we could claim the credit and glory for what we did."

"But we have this treasure in jars of clay to show that this all-surpassing power is from God and not from us" (2 Corinthians 4:7 NIV).

If we could live the Christian life by our own power, then we could claim the credit and glory for what we did. But, because the power to act comes from God, we have no room to boast or brag. Again we see a parallel between our salvation and our Christian walk.

"Salvation is "not of works, lest any man should boast" (Ephesians 2:9).

For the same reason, the power to live godly is not achieved through human effort or works.

One of the most important verses, and best kept secret, concerning the power to live for God is found in Paul's letter to the Galatians.

"I have been crucified with Christ and I no longer live, but Christ lives in me. The life I live in the body, I live by faith in the Son of God, who loved me and gave himself for me" (Galatians 2:20 NIV).

I am dead! How much can a dead man do? Absolutely nothing! But how come I don't feel dead? The answer is simple, the moment we died, God gave us a new life. *"Christ lives in me."*

(Your thoughts, impressions and experiences)

168

CHAPTER TEN
EMPOWERED TO OBEY THE WORD OF GOD

"As long as we hold on to the old self and try to fix it up to make it do the work of God, we are doomed to failure."

God desires to live out the life of Christ in our bodies. Christ's ministry is continuing on earth, finding expression through the lives of the believers.

The only spiritual life in me is Christ's, not mine. So what can we do to gain victory over sin and glorify God after our salvation? Absolutely nothing! Only what God does through us brings glory to God.

There is an old saying that we hear repeated from time to time among believers. "Let go, and let God." Depending upon the context of the action, this philosophy can be right or wrong. The right way to apply this phrase is in letting go of the old self, which was crucified with Christ, and letting God do his work within us.

As long as we hold on to the old self and try to fix it up to make it do the work of God, we are doomed to failure. When we bury the old corpse, and give God the freedom to live his life within us, we experience the power of God in our lives.

HOW MUCH POWER?

There are two verses in the Bible that Christians seem to have a hard time believing. First is,

*"I can
do all things
through Christ who
strengthens me"*
(Philippians 4:13 NKJV).

The word "do" has the idea of divine power to it.

(Your thoughts, impressions and experiences)

"What Paul is saying is that no matter what God brings his way, or allows to come his way, God's power to deal with the circumstances will be sufficient."

The Amplified Bible puts it this way,

"I have strength for all things in Christ Who empowers me—I am ready for anything and equal to anything through Him Who infuses inner strength into me, [that is, I am self-sufficient in Christ's sufficiency]" (Philippians 4:13 AMP).

This verse follows the statement by Paul that he has learned how to be content in every situation of life.

What Paul is saying is that no matter what God brings his way, or allows to come his way, God's power to deal with the circumstances will be sufficient. This is quite a statement, but maybe Paul led a sheltered life. Maybe he never had to experience the big problems you and I face. We get a fairly good idea what Paul's life was like from what he wrote to the Corinthians.

"From the Jews five times I received forty stripes minus one. Three times I was beaten with rods; once I was stoned; three times I was shipwrecked; a night and a day I have been in the deep; in journeys often, in perils of waters, in perils of robbers, in perils of my own countrymen, in perils of the Gentiles, in perils in the city, in perils in the wilderness, in perils in the sea, in perils among false brethren; in weariness and toil, in sleeplessness often, in hunger and thirst, in fastings often, in cold and nakedness. . ." (2 Corinthians 11:24-27 NKJV).

(Your thoughts, impressions and experiences)

CHAPTER TEN
EMPOWERED TO OBEY THE WORD OF GOD

"God says that he will give us enough power to cope with any and every trial and affliction."

Yes, Paul didn't have a life as bad as mine; his life was much worse. Yet he said that in every situation God gave him the power to be content. That is some power.

Since graduating from high school I have lived in eight different states and Puerto Rico. Everywhere I have been, I have met people who had reasons why they could not be content with their circumstances. "It rains too much in Washington." "California has major earthquakes." "Michigan and Wisconsin have tornadoes." "Florida has hurricanes."

Some people are unhappy because they are single, others because they are married. No one has the perfect job or the most pleasant coworkers. No matter how healthy we are, there are always some physical problems.

God says that he will give us enough power to cope with any and every trial and affliction. The unfaithful spouse, the alcoholic parent, whatever the need, God's power will enable us to endure with confidence whatever comes our way. The promise of God's power is even bigger than our daily circumstances and our contentment. The second verse many Christians have a hard time believing is,

"Now to him who is able to do immeasurably more than all we ask or imagine, according to his power that is at work within us"
(Ephesians 3:20 NIV).

God wants to do great things through us!

(Your thoughts, impressions and experiences)

"We can be the remnant, the few who stay faithful to God."

After speaking to a group of pastors, something that in the flesh always brings terror to my heart, a pastor confronted me concerning this verse. "God hasn't exceeded my prayers and hopes," he stated angrily. "In fact, he hasn't even come close to answering some of the smallest requests I have made!" What's the problem? Is it God? Has God promised more than he can deliver? Why doesn't God do more spectacular things in our lives and ministries? The qualifier is found in Ephesians 3:20 NIV, "according to his power that is at work within us."

Those words "according to his power" mean according to the measure of God's power. God's ability to do great and wonderful things in and through us is dependent upon the amount of God's power that we have within us. The pastor who said he never saw God do anything great and wonderful was admitting that he had very little of God's power within him. As we get closer to the end times, more pastors are going to operate without the power of God.

"But mark this:
There will be terrible times
in the last days. People will be
lovers of themselves. . . having
a form of godliness but
denying its power . . ."
(2 Timothy 3:1-2,5 NIV).

Now just because this will be the general condition of the church in the last days doesn't mean that we have to be powerless. We can be the remnant, the few who stay faithful to God.

(Your thoughts, impressions and experiences)

CHAPTER TEN
EMPOWERED TO OBEY THE WORD OF GOD

"As long as we want to act using our own strength, we will be operating without the power of God."

We can experience his power, and to the extent that we do, we will see God do great and wonderful things in and through us.

HOW TO GET GOD'S POWER

God's power comes from God. It is a grace gift and therefore God gives it only to the humble.

*"God
opposes the proud,
but gives grace to
the humble"*
(James 4:6 NIV).

Humility will lead us to acknowledge our complete weakness. Pride will cause us to want to trust our own strength. As long as we want to act using our own strength, we will be operating without the power of God.

Let me illustrate this on a personal level. I have always been a fairly good speaker. I took speech and drama in school, appeared in plays and even had some small parts in a couple of films. My mind is logical and I have the natural ability to arrange information in a logical and simple-to-understand manner. Therefore, when I became a "preacher" I felt I was doing something in an area of my strength. I felt I had every right to see God working through me and my sermons would change the lives of my listeners. But my sermons didn't change lives and I didn't understand why.

By now you understand my problem. I was trying to do the work of the Lord in the energy of the flesh.

(Your thoughts, impressions and experiences)

173

*"The more we yield to
the Holy Spirit, the more we have of his power."*

I thought my strength was sufficient so I didn't really need God's power. I asked God to help me fill in the gaps where my natural ability might have some small flaw. However, it was Cal Bodeutsch performing for God and expecting God to bless him.

One day God spoke to my heart, revealing to me my pride. I had to confess my complete and total dependence upon God. I asked God to give me the words and the sermons that would change lives.

I still studied, I still put my sermon outline together during the week, but I let God lead me through each step of the process. Sometimes it doesn't seem like the sermon really fits together right. Yet, the sermon has been organized not to please me but God. The results of allowing God to lead in every aspect of my sermon preparation have been exciting. I have seen more of God's power in my life, in my sermons and in my efforts to write this book.

Now I am going to repeat myself. Since this is something the Holy Spirit does within us, we must not quench or grieve him. The more we quench the Holy Spirit, the less we have of his power. The more we yield to the Holy Spirit, the more we have of his power. Refer back to chapter six for details on how we hinder the Holy Spirit.

POWER TO PRAY
James expressed the need for God's power in our prayer life,

(Your thoughts, impressions and experiences)

174

CHAPTER TEN
EMPOWERED TO OBEY THE WORD OF GOD

"When the power of God energizes our fervent prayers, we see great results."

"The effective, fervent prayer of a righteous man avails much" (James 5:16 NJKV).

When the power of God energizes our fervent prayers, we see great results. Apart from God's power in our prayers, we can pray all we want and nothing will happen.

Apart from the power of God we do not know how to pray or for what to pray.

"In the same way, the Spirit helps us in our weakness. We do not know what we ought to pray, but the Spirit himself intercedes for us with groans that words cannot express" (Romans 8:26 NIV).

The three words I underlined need further explanation. The word "what" comes from a Greek word that can mean "who, what, how or why." We don't know who to pray for, what to pray for, why to pray or how to pray. Lack of knowledge is our weakness.

The Greek word for "ought" usually is translated "must," as in

"Ye must be born again" (John 3:7).

Our weakness is more than that we don't know how to pray as we should. We don't know how to pray as we must. Therefore, the Holy Spirit comes to our rescue. He "intercedes" for us. This is not a duplication of Christ's ministry as our intercessor today before the Father (Hebrews 7:25).

(Your thoughts, impressions and experiences)

175

"Are you seeing evidences of God's power in your life?"

The word "intercede" means to "meet with to converse." God's Spirit meets with our spirit to eliminate the weakness we have in not knowing how to pray, what to pray, whom to pray for or when to pray for people. The empowering of our prayers comes from God. This is just another area of our spiritual lives where we are dependent upon God's power.

DECISION TIME

Are you seeing evidences of God's power in your life? Are you having victory over sinful habits? Are you experiencing fruit-filled service for God? God wants to do for us above and beyond what we can imagine. But he can only work in proportion to the amount of his power at work within us.

Spend some time in self-examination. Ask God to reveal where pride is blocking God's grace gift of power to you. Ask God to reveal areas of your life where you have not yet yielded yourself to God. When you become aware of these sins, acknowledge them and the harmful effect they have had on your ability to be godly. Thank God for his forgiveness and begin each new day as an opportunity to experience God's power in your life.

(Your thoughts, impressions and experiences)

CHAPTER TEN
QUESTIONS AND DISCUSSION

1. Why don't we have enough personal power to achieve our desires?

_____

_____

_____

_____

2. From where does real power come and how should it be used?

_____

_____

_____

_____

3. What does Galatians 2:20 mean to you?

_____

_____

_____

_____

4. Why must we be dependent upon the Holy Spirit to empower us to be what God wants us to be and do what he wants us to do?

_____

_____

_____

_____

PROJECT

Examine your prayer life. Are you experiencing the power of the Lord to focus your prayers? Spend some time reflecting on your prayers and ask our Lord to enrich them through the Holy Spirit's intercession. Document these thoughts.

CHAPTER ELEVEN
OBEDIENCE TO THE WORD OF GOD

"God wants us to obey him out of love and love cannot be ordered or dictated."

I spoke recently at a church that had just lost their pastor. They had many good things to say about him. He was a great Bible teacher and he had a wonderful family. The one complaint I kept hearing repeatedly was, "He didn't love us." When pressed for details they said, "He was a dictator" or "He was always giving orders or laying down the law to us." It didn't take long for the people to tire of his demands.

Now in all honesty, I have never met the man so I don't know if these observations are true or not, but I have seen pastors who certainly fit this same description. Some pastors view giving commands and following up with threats to be spiritual leadership. In truth, nothing could be further from the truth. Christ didn't walk around threatening people with cosmic annihilation if they didn't follow him or do what he said was right.

God wants us to obey him out of love and love cannot be ordered or dictated. Love is a choice. Manipulation and control remove the ability to choose, and therefore remove the ability to love. But when we are free to choose, we are also free to obey out of love.

Any parent can tell you that obedience motivated by love is a million times better than obedience motivated by fear. Our children can obey us because compared to them, we are bigger, stronger and louder. Or, they can obey us because they see our love for them and in return they love us and want to do that which pleases us.

(Your thoughts, impressions and experiences)

"Legalism can never produce the type of obedience that pleases God."

But before they can choose to obey out of love, we must give them the freedom to make that choice. That means we have to remove the other types of motivation. Fear and guilt-trips are not good motivators because they are not the product of love. The apostle Paul drove home the point that without love our actions have no value, when he wrote,

"If I speak in the tongues of men and of angels, but have not love, I am only a resounding gong or a clanging cymbal. If I have the gift of prophecy and can fathom all mysteries and all knowledge, and if I have a faith that can move mountains, but have not love, I am nothing. If I give all I possess to the poor and surrender my body to the flames, but have not love, I gain nothing" (1 Corinthians 13:1-3 NIV).

Obedience that is not motivated by love is nothing!

Legalism can never produce the type of obedience that pleases God. Under legalism obedience is forced upon people. Under grace obedience is a natural outworking of the Holy Spirit's power within the believer. Legalistic obedience has no real power. About the best one can hope for under legalism is an extended energy of the flesh activity.

Israel serves as a good example of futile, legalistic obedience. After leaving Egypt the Children of Israel came to Mt. Sinai, where God gave Moses the Law, which included the Ten Commandments.

(Your thoughts, impressions and experiences)

180

CHAPTER ELEVEN
OBEDIENCE TO THE WORD OF GOD

"The righteous will live by faith..."

"Moses came and told the people all the words of the Lord, and all the judgments: and all the people answered with one voice, and said, 'All the words which the Lord hath said, will we do'" (Exodus 24:3).

They said they would keep the whole law, every part of it. Did they obey the whole law? No! After giving the law to the people, Moses went back up the mountain to get further instructions from God. Returning down the mountain, Moses finds the children of Israel worshiping a golden calf. Israel was already in gross violation of the law. Why?

Hundreds of years later, after the law was fulfilled by Christ, the apostle Paul would write the Galatian church and explain the real purpose of the law.

"All who rely on observing the law are under a curse, for it is written: 'Cursed is everyone who does not continue to do everything written in the Book of the Law.' Clearly no one is justified before God by the law, because, 'The righteous will live by faith.' What, then, was the purpose of the law? It was added because of transgressions until the Seed to whom the promise referred had come. The law was put into effect through angels by a mediator. . . Is the law, therefore, opposed to the promises of God? Absolutely not! For if a law had been given that could impart life, then righteousness would certainly have come by the law. . .

(Your thoughts, impressions and experiences)

181

"God never intended for the law to be permanent."

Before this faith came, we were held prisoners by the law, locked up until faith should be revealed. So the law was put in charge to lead us to Christ that we might be justified by faith. Now that faith has come, we are no longer under the supervision of the law. It is for freedom that Christ has set us free. Stand firm, then, and do not let yourselves be burdened again by a yoke of slavery" (Galatians 3:10-11,19,21, 24-25; 5:1 NIV).

God never intended for the law to be permanent. He gave it to bring people to the place of seeing they were helpless and hopeless before God. Under the law man was "kept a prisoner," but now we are no longer under the law. We are set free. Part of that freedom is the freedom to choose to love God and obey him. Israel didn't have that choice; they were under a rigid set of rules and punishments. There was a curse upon those who vowed to but did not obey God. They didn't have the permanently indwelling Holy Spirit to give them the desire and power to obey. All the law could do was to restrict negative behavior. The law could not empower proper behavior.

I have been to Promise Keepers. It was an emotional experience for me.

(Your thoughts, impressions and experiences)

182

CHAPTER ELEVEN
OBEDIENCE TO THE WORD OF GOD

"An absence of information on how to keep our promises almost guarantees failure."

Going forward at the end of the conference with thousands of other pastors was a special experience. But, on the first night of the conference when they asked the men to stand up if they were making the seven promises to God, I remained seated. I am sure people wondered about me; what hidden sin prevented me from being "sold out for Christ." But my struggle was on a different plane.

Scripture tells us of the seriousness of making a vow to God.

"So when you talk to God and vow to him that you will do something, don't delay in doing it, for God has no pleasure in fools. Keep your promise to him. It is far better not to say you will do something than to say you will and then not do it" (Ecclesiastes 5:4-5 TLB).

It doesn't matter if it is "ten commandments" or "seven promises;" a vow to obey God is serious.

The question that kept coming to my mind was, "How are they going to try to keep their vows?" Some probably had no idea. They were just caught up in the excitement of the moment and, like the children of Israel, said, "All that you say we will do!" An absence of information on how to keep our promises almost guarantees failure. Energy of the flesh activities are the natural route taken by those who don't understand grace. Perhaps they will add these seven promises to their list of legalistic obligations to God.

(Your thoughts, impressions and experiences)

"Anything and everything we do that does not come from faith is sin and is not pleasing to God."

Perhaps they will depend upon accountability groups to provide the support that only God's Holy Spirit can provide. And when they fail, as fail they must, they will be more discouraged and cynical of Christianity and the Christian life than they ever were before.

I am aware there are those who argue that all obedience is pleasing to God. They say "it doesn't matter if the obedience is motivated by guilt, fear, pressure or love." They quote,

"To obey is better than sacrifice"
(1 Samuel 15:22).

"Obedience to God for any reason is better than disobedience" they affirm. But is "obedience to God" for any reason really obedience?

Let me remind you of two verses we have already looked at.

*"Without faith
it is impossible to
please God"*
(Hebrews 11:6)

and

*"Everything that does
not come from faith is sin"*
(Romans 14:23 NIV).

Anything and everything we do that does not come from faith is sin and is not pleasing to God. Can we obey apart from faith? Yes! The Pharisees were great examples of people who were obedient to the law, but did not have faith.

(Your thoughts, impressions and experiences)

184

CHAPTER ELEVEN
OBEDIENCE TO THE WORD OF GOD

*"Forced obedience may keep us
from suffering the human consequences of our disobedience,
but it does nothing for us spiritually."*

Our Lord's strongest condemnations were directed at the Pharisees.

Which obedience is a product of faith? Is faith found in the man who says, "I will obey God in my own strength," or the man who says, "By the power of the Holy Spirit living within me I can obey God"? The first statement is a clear violation of what God's Word says, and does not please God. The second statement is obedience that comes from faith in what God says. God's work done <u>God's</u> way will always have God's blessing. God's work done <u>man's</u> way will fail to reach its potential in fulfilling God's will.

So is it better to not obey God, than to obey him legalistically? No! Both are sins; both are wrong. Both will rob us of the blessings God gives to those who yield to the Holy Spirit's leading. We like to categorize sins. We have little sins, big sins and really big sins. God just sees sin. <u>Forced obedience may keep us from suffering the human consequences of our disobedience, but it does nothing for us spiritually.</u>

The eighth chapter of Romans deals with our practical sanctification, which is our personal godliness. Listen to what Paul says about how we live for God.

"For what the law could not do in that it was weak through the flesh, God did by sending His own Son in the likeness of sinful flesh, on account of sin:

(Your thoughts, impressions and experiences)

185

" Only those who live in cooperation and submission to the Holy Spirit are going to live righteous lives."

He condemned sin in the flesh, that the righteous requirement of the law might be fulfilled in us who do not walk according to the flesh but according to the Spirit. For those who live according to the flesh set their minds on the things of the flesh, but those who live according to the Spirit, the things of the Spirit. For to be carnally minded is death, but to be spiritually minded is life and peace" (Romans 8:3-6 NKJV).

Only those who live in cooperation and submission to the Holy Spirit are going to live righteous lives. Take away the Holy Spirit, which legalistic obedience to God does, and there is no hope for living a holy life that pleases God. Paul goes on to say,

"And if the spirit of him that raised Jesus from the dead is living in you, he who raised Christ from the dead will also give life to your mortal bodies through his Spirit, who lives in you" (Romans 8:11 NIV).

The life he is speaking about is not our eternal life, for as believers we already have that. The life referred to is the abundant life, the godly life we have as we grow in our relationship with God, the life that comes to us through the Holy Spirit who indwells us!

(Your thoughts, impressions and experiences)

186

CHAPTER ELEVEN
OBEDIENCE TO THE WORD OF GOD

"Obedience is the end result of spiritual growth."

Several times the apostle Paul shared his personal experience in growing in godliness and gave the credit to the grace of God. Paul states,

> *"Now this is our boast: Our conscience testifies that we have conducted ourselves in the world, and especially in our relations with you, in the holiness and sincerity that are from God. We have done so not according to worldly wisdom but according to God's grace"*
> (2 Corinthians 1:12 NIV).

Paul contrasts worldly wisdom with God's grace. Paul's own power or skills did not lead him to obey God. That power source is legalism. No, Paul's conduct was a direct result of living out the grace of God. As Paul had written the Corinthians earlier,

> *"But by the grace of God I am what I am, and his grace to me was not without effect. No, I worked harder than all of them—yet not I, but the grace of God that was with me"*
> (1 Corinthians 15:10 NIV).

We can see the difference between legalism and a grace orientation in what order we put obedience to God. The legalist sees obedience as the first and only step in living the Christian life. Under grace we see obedience is the end result of spiritual growth through personal understanding facilitated by the Holy Spirit of the elements necessary for that growth. We must know the Word of God.

(Your thoughts, impressions and experiences)

"We must have faith that God can and will keep his Word."

We must understand its importance and relevance to our lives. We must have faith that God can and will keep his Word. We must allow the Holy Spirit to place the desire and enabling power within us to obey the Word and then, and only then, can we obey God in a truly spirit-filled way.

True spiritual obedience comes to us by God's grace. All God asks of us is submission to his working within us.

DECISION TIME

God wants you to be obedient to his Word and his will. Is this your desire too? Spend some time talking with God about your commitment to obeying him.

If you are trying to please God through legalistic obedience, now is the time to become free from your bondage. Spend some time talking with God about your desire to obey him, motivated by love and empowered by the Spirit.

(Your thoughts, impressions and experiences)

CHAPTER ELEVEN
QUESTIONS AND DISCUSSION

1. Why must love for God be the motivation of our obedience to him?

   _____

   _____

   _____

2. Why do people make up lists of rules to force people to obey God?

   _____

   _____

   _____

3. How does trying to live the Christian life by a set of rules hinder true spiritual growth?

   _____

   _____

   _____

4. Why can't obedience be the first step in developing our relationship with God?

   _____

   _____

   _____

5. Why did Jesus say such harsh things to the Pharisees?

_____

_____

_____

_____

6. Under grace, how does obedience to God become a reality?

_____

_____

_____

_____

PROJECT

Reflect upon instances in your life where your relationship with God has been based on legalistic rules or behavior. Indicate those instances where you put obedience to rules as the first aspect of your spiritual relationship. Write a paragraph discussing how to achieve your desire to grow spiritually.

_____

_____

_____

_____

_____

_____

_____

_____

CHAPTER TWELVE
BIGGER THAN OBEDIENCE

"Paul was laboring diligently with a goal in mind that believers might become like Christ, not just become obedient Christians."

According to the legalistic paradigm, the Christian life begins and ends with obedience. Legalism assumes the total sum of the Christian experience is obedience to God. Obedience is not just one aspect of our relationship with God, it is everything to the legalist. God wants us to experience much more. Just as parents want more in their relationship with their children than mere obedience, so too does our heavenly Father.

CHRISTLIKENESS

The apostle Paul, in expressing his desire for the believers in Galatia, said,

*"My dear children, for whom
I am again in the pains of childbirth until
Christ is formed in you"*
(Galatians 4:19 NIV).

Paul was laboring diligently with a goal in mind that believers might become like Christ, not just become obedient Christians. The formation of the virtues of Christ within the believer exceeds mere obedience. Christlikeness deals with what we become as Christians. Obedience deals with what we do.

"Christ in you" is different from "us in Christ." The moment God saved us, we were placed into the church, the body of Christ, by the Holy Spirit.

*"For by one Spirit are we all baptized
into one body, whether we
be Jews or Gentiles, whether we
be bond or free; and have been
all made to drink into
one Spirit"*
(1 Corinthians 12:13).

(Your thoughts, impressions and experiences)

"Christ formed in you" is the goal of spiritual growth."

A study of the words "in Christ" throughout Paul's epistles shows that all of the blessings we receive as believers come to us because we are "in Christ." Being in Christ is something that happened at the time of our salvation. We call this doctrine "positional truth" because it deals with what is true of our standing, or position, as Christians. If "Christ formed in you" were the same as us "in Christ," then Paul would not have labored so hard for this change to happen in the life of believers; Christlikeness would have already happened at the time of salvation. Nor is "Christ formed in you" the same as the Holy Spirit within us.

"What? know ye not that your body is the temple of the Holy Ghost which is in you, which ye have of God, and ye are not your own?"
(1 Corinthians 6:19).

This is the doctrine of the indwelling Holy Spirit. The moment God saved us the Holy Spirit came to live within us. The doctrine of the indwelling Holy Spirit is also a positional truth.

"Christ formed in you" is the goal of spiritual growth. When we begin to think like Christ, feel like Christ and act as Christ acted, then we are Christlike. As the Word of God transforms our minds, our lives become transfigured into the image of Christ.

"And be not conformed to this world: but be ye transformed by the renewing of your mind, that ye may prove what is that good, and acceptable, and perfect, will of God"
(Romans 12:2).

(Your thoughts, impressions and experiences)

192

CHAPTER TWELVE
BIGGER THAN OBEDIENCE

"Paul's highest goal was for God to change him into the image of Christ."

When God changes us into the image of Christ, we can live out God's will for our lives.

Paul's highest goal was for God to change him into the image of Christ.

"According to my earnest expectation and my hope, that in nothing I shall be ashamed, but that with all boldness, as always, so now also Christ shall be magnified in my body, whether it be by life or by death," (Philippians 1:20).

The word "magnified" means to be made visible and enlarged. Paul wanted people to see Christ in everything he did. He wanted to be more like Christ and show forth Christ to others.

Christlikeness was also a major focus of Paul's prayers for believers.

"That Christ may dwell in your hearts by faith; that ye, being rooted and grounded in love, May be able to comprehend with all saints what is the breadth, and length, and depth, and height; And to know the love of Christ, which passeth knowledge, that ye might be filled with all the fulness of God" (Ephesians 3:17-19).

The word "dwell" is not the same word for "indwell." This "dwell" means Christ should be at home and able to influence our lives. Christ wants to influence our daily actions and decisions..

(Your thoughts, impressions and experiences)

193

"The Holy Spirit of God and the holy Word of God produce the holy child of God."

Verse nineteen states the result of Christ influencing our thoughts, attitudes and behavior. God himself will fill us with "all the fulness of God." Since Christ is the fulness of God (Colossians 2:9), when we are filled with all the fulness of God we are filled with Christ.

The apostle Paul speaks of the mystery in the epistle to the Colossians. This mystery, or secret, is the truth of what God seeks to accomplish through believers today. The mystery deals with the church's responsibilities and promises from God. Paul addresses the idea of Christlikeness when he states,

"Even the mystery which hath been hid from ages and from generations, but now is made manifest to his saints: To whom God would make known what is the riches of the glory of this mystery among the Gentiles; which is Christ in you, the hope of glory"
(Colossians 1:26-27).

"Christ in you" is the riches of the glory of what God wants to do with the church today, not you in Christ, not the Holy Spirit in you, but Christ in you.

How do we become Christlike? Christlikeness is only possible through the working of the Holy Spirit and the Word of God. The Holy Spirit of God and the holy Word of God produce the holy child of God. We must know, understand and believe the Word of God. We must allow the Holy Spirit to give us the desire and power to obey the Word of God.

(Your thoughts, impressions and experiences)

194

CHAPTER TWELVE
BIGGER THAN OBEDIENCE

"God wants our love, not just our obedience."

Unless we yield to the working of the Holy Spirit through the Word of God, we will never become Christlike.

LOVING GOD

God wants us to love him! When the lawyer asked Jesus what was the greatest law, we read,

"Jesus said unto him, Thou shalt love the Lord thy God with all thy heart, and with all thy soul, and with all thy mind" (Matthew 22:37).

He did not say, "Thou shalt obey the Lord thy God with all thy heart, and with all thy soul, and with all thy mind." The Pharisees of Jesus' day tried to obey the whole law, religiously, but their obedience was not pleasing to God. God wants our love, not just our obedience.

God's desire that we love him is the cause of all the evil in the world. Yes, that's right! If God did not want our love, he would have made us more like robots than people with free will. God created the human race so that we could love him. Love cannot be forced. We can only give love freely.

For us to be able to love God, we must be able to choose. Therefore, God created us with the freedom to choose to love him. However, along with the freedom to choose to love him there is also the freedom to choose not to love him. Man, using his free will, chose to turn away from God and to sin instead. We experience evil in the world because God gave us the freedom to choose to love him.

(Your thoughts, impressions and experiences)

195

CHAPTER TWELVE
BIGGER THAN OBEDIENCE

"God's love for us caused Christ to go to the cross."

God's desire that we love him is the cause of the cross of Christ. Most people are familiar with John 3:16,

"For God so loved the world, that he gave his only begotten Son, that whosoever believeth in him should not perish, but have everlasting life" (John 3:16).

God's love for us caused Christ to go to the cross. This truth is the heart of the gospel. Christ's death on the cross is God's greatest demonstration of love. When sin entered the world, it blocked our ability to love God. In order for us to love God, he had to remove the obstacle of sin. Only after we have experienced the forgiveness of God for our sin are we able to love him. God's desire for us to love him is so great that he was willing to send his beloved Son to the cross.

What does it look and feel like to love God? How will I know when I love God? Let us consider two answers, although I am sure there are many more possibilities. First, loving God looks and feels like loving anyone else. Jesus said,

"If ye love me, keep my commandments" (John 14:15).

Jesus does not use the word for obeying in this verse. The Greek word for "keep" means to guard or hold onto. This verse is saying that those who love Christ will hold onto what he says.

I can still remember when I was a teenager. I would send and receive "love notes" from the flame of the month.

(Your thoughts, impressions and experiences)

CHAPTER TWELVE
BIGGER THAN OBEDIENCE

"Only love can produce the desire for obedience to God."

It was always exciting to get a new note to read and reread all day. I would "hold onto" every word. That action is the idea Jesus is expressing in John 14:15. Two people in love will hold onto every word spoken by the object of their affection. When the object of our affection is God, we will hold onto (keep) his words.

Second, loving God is a pleasurable experience. If love were not so pleasurable, we would not be so excited about love and desirous to find it.

Every little girl's dream is to fall in love with her handsome prince and live happily ever after. Every boy's dream is to receive his girl's love with physical affection. Why do people want to fall in love? Is it not because we want to experience the emotional and physical pleasure we associate with love?

Loving God should be a pleasurable experience. If we are not enjoying our relationship with God something is wrong! Of all the things Jesus could have said that made up the very heart of God's desire for humanity, he didn't say to fear God or serve God with all our heart, soul and mind. Jesus said to love God. Therefore, I have to believe that because love is pleasurable, God wants our experience with him to be pleasurable, too.

Legalism cannot produce love. Legalism can't even give us power to obey. Legalism might try to force us to obey, but it can't make us want to obey God. Only love can produce the desire for obedience to God. No wonder God created us to love him!

(Your thoughts, impressions and experiences)

"Those who have never entered into a personal relationship with God through Christ Jesus cannot bring glory to God."

Along with love comes everything else, including all the gifts God wants to give us to bring real and sustained spiritual, emotional and physical pleasure to our lives..

GLORIFYING GOD
God wants us to glorify him.

*"Whether therefore ye eat,
or drink, or whatsoever ye do, do all to
the glory of God"*
(1 Corinthians 10:31).

Glorifying God is the ultimate goal of all that the believer says or does.

A few years ago I taught a six-month class on Christian Ethics. The first three months we explored and analyzed different ethical systems, seeking to identify the uniqueness of the Christian ethic. This was our conclusion: the Christian ethic is different from all other ethical systems in that life's ultimate objective is to glorify God through Christ Jesus.

Those who have never entered into a personal relationship with God through Christ Jesus cannot bring glory to God. How can the Bible say of the unsaved,

*"They are all gone out of the way,
they are together become unprofitable;
there is none that doeth good,
no, not one"*
(Romans 3:12).

I know many unsaved individuals who are good people and do many good things. So how can God say "there is none that doeth good, no, not one?"

(Your thoughts, impressions and experiences)

CHAPTER TWELVE
BIGGER THAN OBEDIENCE

"Christians have the potential of glorifying God, but often do not."

Ethicists tell us that in order for something to be good, three criteria must be met. First, the ends must be good. We must be seeking to do something kind or beneficial, not evil or harmful. Second, the means must be good. As Bob Jones, Sr. used to say, "It is never right to do a wrong to do a right." Good ends never justify evil means. Third, the motive must be good. According to God's Word there is only one good motive. We are to do all to the glory of God.

Unsaved people cannot do "good" because they fall short on the third criterion. The ends they accomplish can be good. The means may also be good, but the motive is not to bring glory to God through Christ Jesus. Therefore, the good things they do are done with the wrong motive and no longer meet God's standard of what is good.

Christians have the potential of glorifying God, but often do not. Often the flesh motivates Christians. Then the good that they would do is not pleasing to God,

*"So then
they that are in the flesh
cannot please God"*
(Romans 8:8).

Christians can "serve the Lord" with the right ends and means, but with the wrong motive and by that, their good works are no longer good in the eyes of God.

Usually we frown on people who seek glory for themselves. Glory seekers are conceited bores.

(Your thoughts, impressions and experiences)

"God deals with us according to his grace."

So how can God want us to give him glory? Why is it good for him and bad for us? Individuals who seek glory for themselves forget all the people who are responsible for their success. No man or woman can take complete credit for any success or achievement.

The creation of this book is a great example. God gave me the intellect and the good health to enable me to write. God gave me the spiritual insight to know the subject matter. God gave discernment to the publishers, without whom this would be just a pile of papers on top of my filing cabinet. In every way this book is a work of God. God didn't have to use me to write this book. I was just available and willing. God chose me, by his grace, to be the finger on the keyboard.

Taking credit for this book would be wrong. Taking credit for his creation would not be wrong for God; therefore, the glory rightly belongs to him.

God is dependent upon no one. He created the world by the power of his Word. He saves us by his grace. God deserves the glory because he is indebted to no one. Only God is worthy of glory.

God's power and grace make up his glory. God is all-powerful, omnipotent. God can do anything that is good. God deals with us according to his grace. There is nothing good that he will not do for us. We cannot glory in ourselves because our power and grace cannot compare to God's. We are weak and frail compared to God.

(Your thoughts, impressions and experiences)

200

CHAPTER TWELVE
BIGGER THAN OBEDIENCE

"Pride keeps us from acknowledging our helplessness."

God made us weak and frail so that we might glory in his working within us.

"And base things of the world, and things which are despised, hath God chosen, yea, and things which are not, to bring to nought things that are: That no flesh should glory in his presence. But of him are ye in Christ Jesus, who of God is made unto us wisdom, and righteousness, and sanctification, and redemption: That, according as it is written, He that glorieth, let him glory in the Lord" (1 Corinthians 1:28-31).

Pride keeps us from acknowledging our helplessness. Pride, therefore, keeps us from glorifying God. Legalism focuses on our personal strength to live the Christian life. Legalism also keeps us from glorifying God. The Pharisees obeyed God legalistically, but they did not glorify God. God wants us to glorify him, something much bigger than mere obedience.

ENJOYING GOD

The Shorter Westminster Confession asks, "What is the purpose of man?" The answer given is, "The purpose of man is to glorify God and enjoy him forever." Try this experiment sometime. Ask Christians to fill in the blank, "God wants me to _____ him." Most Christians will say either love, serve or obey. I have never yet had anyone volunteer the word "enjoy." Nevertheless, God does want us to enjoy him.

What does it mean "to enjoy God?" How do we enjoy the almighty God, creator of all?

(Your thoughts, impressions and experiences)

201

"God has some wonderful gifts to give us."

First, we enjoy him by enjoying his creation. When the Children of Israel first possessed the Promised Land, Joshua gave this admonition to them.

"Until the LORD have given your brethren rest, as he hath given you, and they also have possessed the land which the LORD your God giveth them: then ye shall return unto the land of your possession, and enjoy it, which Moses the LORD's servant gave you on this side Jordan toward the sunrising"
(Joshua 1:15).

In enjoying what God gave them, Israel was enjoying God.

Paul told his son in the faith, Timothy,

"Charge them that are rich in this world, that they be not high-minded, nor trust in uncertain riches, but in the living God, who giveth us richly all things to enjoy"
(1 Timothy 6:17).

We can enjoy God like we might enjoy a generous friend or relative. When I was a kid, I had a rich aunt and uncle (they never had any children). I always enjoyed going to their house. I knew that on my birthday or Christmas I would get something really enjoyable from them. They never disappointed me. God has some wonderful things to give us.

"Every good gift and every perfect gift is from above, and cometh down from the Father of lights, with whom is no variableness, neither shadow of turning"
(James 1:17).

(Your thoughts, impressions and experiences)

202

CHAPTER TWELVE
BIGGER THAN OBEDIENCE

"I enjoy God because God enjoys me."

I can count on receiving good gifts from God. I am assured by my loving relationship with him that he will never disappoint me. I can enjoy God as I enjoy all the wonderful blessings he gives me.

We can enjoy God on a deeper level than just enjoying what he gives us. I enjoy God because God enjoys me. God likes me! He likes me with all my faults and failings.

My performance or appearance will never cause God to reject me. Yes, God will transform me into Christlikeness as I grow spiritually, but that doesn't change the fact that he also likes me just as I am.

Some people are always pushing us to improve. I heard a nationally-known speaker say he always pushed his children to do better. If they got a C on their report card, it wasn't good enough. Neither was a B, A-, A.

Even if they got an A+ he would find another area for them to improve. His reasoning was that he didn't want his children to be satisfied or content with what they were. He wanted to motivate them to improve and to be better than they were. I had one thought as I listened to him, "Thank God I was not his child."

People like this speaker may have the right motive, but the message we get is, "We are not good enough for them." If the person is someone we perceive as important, a parent or perhaps a teacher or coach, we begin to resent them. We don't enjoy being with them.

(Your thoughts, impressions and experiences)

*"Some Christians cannot enjoy
God and the Christian life because they aren't perfect yet."*

Some people drive themselves to constantly improve different areas of their life. These unhappy people are always working on something. Yet once their self-improvement project is over, they still aren't happy with themselves. Well-meaning pastors have taught Christians that they need to change in order for God to hear their prayers or answer their cries for help. Pastors are really driving these people away from God. Pastors would do better if they helped their congregations to enjoy God first.

A legalistic paradigm will never lead us to enjoy God. Legalists don't even know that God wants us to enjoy him. If people are obsessing over the rules, they will never enjoy their relationship with God.

When I was in elementary school, I started playing a musical instrument. I played it all the way through high school in the school band. I really enjoyed playing it. I still have that instrument and play it from time to time, but not with the same enjoyment. The reason is that I am so out of practice, I must concentrate very hard to play the notes and rhythm correctly. Since my focus is on doing it right, I can't enjoy the process.

The same is true with Christians. Some Christians cannot enjoy God and the Christian life because they aren't perfect yet. If we wait to enjoy God until we are perfect, we will not enjoy God in this lifetime!

I am not saying we shouldn't be obedient to God.

(Your thoughts, impressions and experiences)

CHAPTER TWELVE
BIGGER THAN OBEDIENCE

"Do you desire to live a life that goes beyond mere obedience?"

The bulk of this book discusses how to be biblically obedient to God. What I am saying is that there is much more to the Christian life than just obeying God! Legalism is not the road we want to travel if we want to receive God's best gifts for our lives. Only God's grace brings us all we want and need when we truly trust God and seek him with humility in our hearts.

I pray Christ will be formed in you and that you will continue to develop a loving relationship with our Father in heaven that will glorify him and manifest itself with great joy in your life.

"The grace of our Lord Jesus Christ be with you all. Amen"
(Romans 16:24).

DECISION TIME
Are you committed to the paradigm of grace? Do you desire to live a life that goes beyond mere obedience? Decide today which path toward godliness you choose to take. Tell God of your heart's desire.

(Your thoughts, impressions and experiences)

CHAPTER TWELVE
QUESTIONS AND DISCUSSION

1. Discuss the difference between the two truths "you in Christ" and "Christ formed in you."

    _____

    _____

    _____

    _____

2. Explain what becoming transformed to Christlikeness means to you. How do Christians become Christlike?

    _____

    _____

    _____

    _____

3. Discuss what your God-given freedom to choose to love God means to you. List areas in your life where your choices do not properly reflect the holy person you desire to be. Pray about these areas, asking God to help you make better choices. Discuss the role of the Holy Spirit in this process.

    _____

    _____

    _____

    _____

4. Only after we have experienced the forgiveness of God for our sin are we able to truly love him. What does this statement mean to you?

    _____

    _____

    _____

5. What does it look and feel like to love God?

_____

_____

_____

_____

6. The Christian ethic is different from all other ethical systems in that life's ultimate objective is to glorify God through Jesus Christ. Discuss how the good works you do may be done with the wrong motive and no longer meet God's standard of what is good.

_____

_____

_____

_____

7. God chose you by his grace. Therefore, the glory for all that you do rightly belongs to him. Discuss what this concept means to you.

_____

_____

_____

_____

8. How does pride keep us from acknowledging our helplessness and glorifying God?

_____

_____

_____

_____

_____

9. What does it mean to enjoy God? How does a legalistic paradigm inhibit our ability to enjoy God?

_____

_____

_____

_____

PROJECT

Reflect upon the lessons learned from this book. Write a short summarization of the key concepts from each chapter. Discuss what each concept means to you and the impact this understanding can have upon your spiritual growth. Pray for a deeper, loving relationship with our Father and the power to glorify him throughout your life.

_____

_____

_____

_____

_____

_____

_____

_____

_____

_____

_____

ADDITIONAL JOURNALING

THE
GRACE
WAY...

*A*re you interested in using
THE GRACE WAY for a group?

Check with Grace Publications
for special volume prices.